ANCHORING INTO GRACE

A step-by-step guide to breaking free from chronic stress & feeling calm in a chaotic world

BELLA DODDS

LUMINARIES PUBLISHING

LUMINARIES PUBLISHING
PO Box 724
Boulder, CO 80306

Cover Image: Klagyivik Viktor/shutterstock.com

1. Mind and body   2. Spiritual well-being   3. Self-care

ISBN (print) 978-0-9839836-2-0

1st Luminaries Publishing edition, June 2021

For my mom, dad, and grandmother.
Without your unconditional love and support,
this book could not have been written.

Contents

1

Everything I share in this book I have been through myself.

I know how exhausting and overwhelming it can feel to try to hold everything together and to stay on top of all your responsibilities, but despite your best efforts, either someone is frustrated with you at work or at home, you're running behind with everything you need to get done, a family member gets sick, an unexpected bill comes in, your kids are struggling, a global pandemic erupts—that no matter how hard you are trying, there is always some new problem robbing you of your ability to feel calm, happy, or at ease for very long.

I know what it is like to walk on eggshells around your partner, trying to say the right thing to avoid another argument. To wake up in the morning and before your feet even hit the floor, your mind races and your chest tightens thinking of everything you've got to get done. I know what it is like to go through your day prodded by a hot iron rod of urgency, with an endless to-do list making you feel like you're constantly behind (even though you're working so hard). I understand how overwhelming it can be to process the ever-increasing crises in the world. I know what it is like to need more time, but you don't have more time. To need more energy, but you don't have more energy. Juggling it all may leave you wondering: If I'm working so hard … why isn't my life running more smoothly? If I'm doing my best … why am I not happier?

What I will teach you in *Anchoring into Grace* is a much-needed solution to relentless stress by understanding **why you are stuck in overdrive in the first place (the reason is not often what most people think).**

This book will not approach daily frustrations and burnout merely from an intellectual perspective, nor solely through calming exercises. I will offer a combination of both *because you need both.* You need to understand why you are defaulting into tension and strain just going about your normal day, and equally why all of your efforts aren't producing the results you want. When you understand the underlying problem, you can focus on the solution, learning how to manage your workload with greater ease and efficiency *and* how to feel more calm and energized as you go about your busy day.

The process I'v developed and what I want to teach you is what I used to heal myself after a deeply painful and strenuous period in my life. Five family members had passed away, two others were diagnosed with cancer, and a loved one was struggling with late stages of alcoholism, all while I was in the middle of a painful breakup, struggling with a back injury, and of course, was still juggling all of my daily responsibilities. It was at my rock bottom when I realized that what I was doing to try and hold it all together and make sure that everyone and everything around me was okay ... was obviously not working.

In the face of so much challenge, I reached a breaking point where it all became too much, and during the height of a particularly painful experience I knew in that moment the only wise choice left was to surrender ...

Thankfully, through surrender came grace and not long after, a beautiful, higher path emerged that changed the trajectory of my life.

It took time to thread the various pieces together to discover how I was working against myself in ways I didn't realize and how to make key shifts in order for my best intentions to get *far better results*. But in time, what I pieced together along this path is what I used to change my life and heal myself, and how I have since helped people from around the world to do the same.

In sharing this process with my clients, it has allowed them to have a clear understanding of what was keeping them stuck in relentless stress, while simultaneously providing logical insights into exactly why all of their hard work wasn't producing the results they wanted. In a short period of time, client after client was able to interrupt decades-long patterns of being tightly wound—and replace overworking themselves with handling their lives and workloads more effectively—and with greater joy and inner peace. They also became aware of their innate strengths and how to use their strengths more masterfully to get higher quality outcomes in their lives.

The process I took them through equally freed up the inner resistance they held in connecting to and embodying their intrinsic worth. Before I began using this approach, what once took months for my clients to be able to feel genuine love and appreciation for themselves (if they would ever fully get there), began to happen naturally and with a deep, authentic know-ingness. From here they were able to rest and be replenished in deeper levels of peace, which created an acceleration in their healing journeys as well as a renewal of joy and meaning in their lives.

And now I want to share this process with you.

In writing this book, my goals for you are:

- to help you replace the blood, sweat, and tear approach to life by working smart, not hard.
- to empower you to own your unique strengths and use your gifts in balanced healthy ways (so that you don't unintentionally work against yourself).
- to help you understand why some of your efforts are falling short, no matter how hard you are trying.
- to teach you how to shift out of an exhausting, gripping, control mindset and into an empowered, fulfilling growth mindset.
- to help you learn how to tap into a source of peace that is available to you at all times, even when there is chaos going on around you.
- to help you live from the inside out, rather than the outside in (you will understand exactly what I mean by this by the end of this book).
- to help you understand and value yourself in ways you perhaps haven't in years (if ever).
- to teach you how to connect to your inner healer and to feel the depth and stunning beauty of who you really are.
- to help you embody deeper levels of peace and love within you so that you may experience renewed levels of joy, inspiration, connection, and purpose in your life.

To meet these goals, we must look at what is keeping you stuck in unnecessarily high-stress levels just going about your normal day-to-day responsibilities—as well as dive into why all of your efforts aren't producing the results you want—and from there we can focus on a transformative solution.

Before we can talk about the solution, a core problem we need to solve is how to reverse your:

Overactive Survival Stress Response

What exactly is your survival stress response?
Your body has a survival program (which is also known as your fight, flight, freeze response). This program is a highly advanced system and its main purpose is to keep you safe and alive. One of the ways it does this is by constantly scanning your environment to make sure everything around you is safe and secure.

When you experience a situation, big or small, that is not to your liking, within seconds this can alert your survival program to trigger a cascade of biological events inside you—including an increase in your heart rate, blood pressure, blood sugar levels, and stress hormones—all for the purpose of giving you a burst of energy to overcome the immediate problem. This is not bad in and of itself. But if your survival program is being chronically triggered throughout the day, this can result in a painful, exhausting way to live (not to mention being incredibly harmful to your physical health).

What does it mean when your survival mode is overactive?
Your survival program becomes overactive when it is chronically switched on or is triggered throughout your day by non-life-threatening situations.

What are some signs that your survival mode is overactive?
Any of the following can be signs that your survival mode

is overactive: feeling overly tense, anxious, or frustrated just going about your day; feeling overwhelmed or frozen when you think of everything you have to get done; feeling chronically exhausted or burnt out; having difficulty concentrating; feeling empty, disconnected, or depressed; being ridden with guilt or being overly hard on yourself; feeling like you can't make a mistake or disappoint someone; stewing about something mentally and emotionally and being unable to stop; experiencing weekly arguments with your partner; having difficulty sleeping; worrying that something bad might happen; not feeling like yourself anymore; craving comfort foods, alcohol, or binge-watching television on a regular basis as the only way to switch off; being unable to rest and relax deeply for long before tension starts creeping back in again.

> Physical signs can include struggling with chronic health problems such as: stubborn weight, chronic pain, headaches, IBS, ulcers, food allergies, brain fog, hormonal imbalances, fertility challenges, eczema, adrenal fatigue, autoimmune diseases, diabetes, high blood pressure, etc.

Now, take a nice deep breath in …

And exhale.

This book will lead you on an empowering journey of self-discovery in understanding why your survival stress response is being triggered throughout the day—and it will also offer a solution. (Thankfully, the solution is beautiful and can bring new meaning, depth, and beauty to your life.)

In order to self-heal your overactive stress response, we need to break it down and get crystal clear on **what is**

really going on underneath the surface. It is actually quite eye-opening when you get to the heart of the problem, and it is essential that you address the underlying issue—because no matter how hard you intellectually try to force yourself to stop worrying, let go, and relax as you go about your normal day—**your body's survival program won't let you**.

There is a reason you are struggling under a pressure cooker's worth of stress just going about your normal day.

There is a reason you feel anxious, frustrated, or overwhelmed.

There is a reason you can't relax or feel good for any length of time before the all-too-familiar tension and worry creeps back in again.

It isn't because 'you're not good at juggling it all,' or because that's 'just life.' Rather, it's because the primary function of your body's hyper-vigilant survival program is to keep you alive, which essentially means that your body and mind have a very hard time letting go and allowing you to feel calm when everything around you is not 100% solved, in place, in order, and okay. But since that will never happen (especially in the fast-paced, complex 21st century world), you need a new, upgraded way of navigating the world as you juggle your many roles and responsibilities—a way of moving through the world that brings out the best in you, rather than exhausts, overwhelms, depletes, or frustrates you.

In *Anchoring into Grace* I am not coming from the perspective that you and your body are making a mistake by defaulting into survival mode—I am coming from the understanding that if you are experiencing chronically high-stress levels just going about your normal day—**there is a reason.**

In honoring who you are on all levels, I have been dedicated to figuring out what that reason is. And I have found an important piece in the mindbody healing puzzle.

In order to teach you how to reverse your overactive survival stress response and increase your capacity to relax, feel better, and manage your workload more effectively, I have broken this book down into three logical, easy-to-read sections:

Section One: **The Foundation**

In this section, I will introduce to you why your nervous system naturally defaults into survival mode and how you can work with your body's survival program in order to feel good, be more relaxed, and embody a sense of calm going about your normal day-to-day.

Section Two: **The Discovery**

In this section, you will learn that it is directly out of your survival stress response where you first developed some of your greatest strengths. In understanding the origins of your strengths and how your abilities have served you throughout your life, you will learn how to use your strengths in balanced, healthy ways (so as not to work against yourself or to unintentionally default into chronic stress throughout the day).

Section Three: **The Solution**

In this section, you will learn how to connect to an *ocean of peace* that is always available to you, and you will learn how to replenish yourself mentally, emotionally, physically, and spiritually each day. You will also learn how to connect to yourself on a Soul Level and feel the depth and beauty of who you really are.

As you begin to understand *why* your body and mind are running at such high-stress levels, you will realize that there is not something wrong with you—your body's survival program is simply doing what it was designed to do. Understanding the positive intentions of your survival program will enable you to begin working in harmony with it, helping you to work smarter, not harder, and strengthening your ability to be more calm, present, and energized as you go through the day—all of which will help you to be better equipped to handle the demands and pace of 21st century life.

How To Use This Book

I encourage you to approach *Anchoring into Grace* with the understanding that each chapter will build on the one prior, revealing a new layer that will enable you to shift out of chronic stress and have your life run more smoothly as you feel more peaceful and strong inside yourself. You will find exercises in almost every chapter, and it is important to know that *you do not need to do these exercises perfectly* in order to teach your body how to anchor into peace. As you go through the book, be kind to yourself as you learn to integrate these new principles; be curious and open to discovering new levels within yourself; stick with the process as you peel away the layers of what is keeping you stuck in relentless stress … and your efforts can be bountifully rewarded.

This book greatly complements other healing practices such as mindfulness, meditation, yoga, and traditional therapies, as well as offering invaluable insights if you are healing your codependency through Al-Anon or ACA meetings. If you are working with a holistic health doctor or practitioner, the step-by-step process within this book can equally support the work you are doing to address your stress-related health problems. It can also significantly deepen your connection to a loving, spiritual energy of your own understanding.

If you are agnostic or an atheist, you can derive equal value from this book as will those who have spiritual beliefs. Why? Because we will be working with the universal healing energies of peace, connection, love, and joy—so please frame these emotional states in how they bring richness, value, and meaning to your own life.

What we do know, based on countless scientific studies, is that there is incontrovertible evidence that our bodies' innate healing capacity is supported when we experience higher emotional states of tranquility. In a peaceful, homeostatic state, our brainwaves slow down, our blood pressure and heart rates decrease, and our parasympathetic nervous systems go into heal and repair mode.

Therefore, I will reference the energies of peace, love, and joy as healing and spiritual energies, as after two decades of working in the healing arts, I humbly understand all of these energies to be one and the same. Love heals us. Love is the transcendent presence that connects us to one another. Within this beautiful, wise-awakened presence is a quality that far surpasses any words we could use to describe it, and it has the ability to harmonize our heart, mind, and body with grace.

In *Anchoring into Grace*, I will teach you how to tap into an ocean of love and peace that is available to you at all times and how to connect to this calming energy in a practical, reproducible way. Once you learn how to access these healing energies more easily, instead of feeling burnt out and depleted at the end of each day, you will be able to replenish yourself throughout the day and enjoy your life on a new level.

With that said, let's dive in!

The first question to ask in order to work in harmony with the wisdom of your mind and body is:

What is REALLY triggering my overactive survival stress response?

Author's Note:
This book can be invaluable for readers who are struggling with exhaustion, depletion, or overwhelm, facing conflicts in relationships, being overly hard on themselves, or experiencing chronically high stress levels. However, if you have experienced high levels of trauma or are currently struggling with PTSD, anxiety, depression, or other mental health challenges, please be aware that in some of the exercises we will be working with your mental and emotional triggers. While for some readers this can be an illuminating, empowering process, for others it may be too triggering. If at any time you find the exercises in this book to be too challenging, you can simply jump to *The Solution Section* to learn how to practice connecting to an ocean of peace that is always available to you.

Section One:
The Foundation

In this section you will learn why your nervous system is defaulting into survival mode and why it is so difficult to relax and feel calm just going about your normal day.

2

What is REALLY triggering my overactive survival stress response?

During our initial consultation, Megan expressed the reasons she was reaching out for help. As she conveyed her story, there was a clear tone of exhaustion, sadness, and angst in her voice:

> "I feel overwhelmed most of the time. My life has become a constant whirlwind between managing everything with the kids and trying to stay on top of everything at work. Every day, from the moment I wake up until I go to sleep, I'm constantly busy … but somehow, I still feel behind or that I always have more to do. My husband and I haven't been getting along great. We're constantly pushing each other's buttons. It makes me sad to say this, but my life is starting to feel like an endless drudge. I'm exhausted. My stress is starting to get the best of me … I'm losing my patience with my kids. It's been a long time since I felt happy. I don't know what to do or how long I can keep going at this pace …"

I understood where Megan was coming from wholeheartedly. Not only could I personally relate, having endured tremendous hardships years prior, but the majority of clients I work with each week are struggling with challenges similar to Megan's.

And this is why I wrote *Anchoring into Grace*. The material I'm going to share with you took me years to piece together—but my hope is that in reading this book—you will be able to start implementing these life-changing insights into your own life within a matter of weeks.

We are going to go over quite a bit of information in the next few pages. As a heads-up, I will be teaching chapter 2 with a direct and straightforward tone (but this is by no means how the rest of the book will read). My approach is a balance of logic and heart-felt emotions, of matter-of-factness and calm serenity. The majority of information and steps within in this book are empowering and inspiring—but to get to the momentous chapters—at the beginning we have to address the core issues triggering the overactive stress response. Some of the information in this chapter might be a bit heavy to read—or it could be the opposite—it could fill you with a sense of relief, igniting light bulbs to go off in your mind. In either respect, it is essential to understand why your body and mind keep pulling you into tension and hypervigilance just going about your normal day, so that you can get off the hamster wheel and start seeing all your efforts produce far better results.

With this in mind, for the next two chapters, I recommend approaching this material with a growth mindset—meaning you are **determined** and **ready** to understand the root problem—so that you can focus on what is in your control and what you can do to improve the quality of your life. Please bear with me as I create a solid foundation right from the get-go, as I will be building on these concepts in greater depth throughout the rest of the book. For this reason, I suggest coming back to this chapter as often as you need to.

In this chapter, we'll be exploring:

1. The two most common stress patterns that trigger the overactive survival stress response.
2. Evolutionary dependency and what differentiates it from codependency.

Let's dive right in and start with number one and investigate the two most common stress patterns triggering the overactive survival stress response.

Since 2010, I've had an international holistic health coaching practice. What I've discovered in this time, and in working with people from around the world, is that regardless of my clients' differences in culture, race, socioeconomic status, age, gender, sexual orientation—whether they were from the United States, England, Greece, Russia, Scotland, Australia, Italy, South Africa, Sweden, Argentina, Canada, or Mexico; or if their spiritual beliefs were Christian, Muslim, Catholic, Sikh, Mormon, Jehovah's Witness, Buddhist, Hindu, agnostic, atheist, or Spiritual but not religious—despite the wide range of differences in their backgrounds—**there were two acute stress patterns that all of my clients shared in common**.

Discovering this commonality from such a diverse group of people was like seeing a big flashing neon sign that said:

You have arrived at an important piece of the puzzle ... do not rush ahead.

So I didn't rush over it. Rather, I dove in deeper to uncover the ripple effect from these two stress patterns, and I spent years honing in on a solution that would work in harmony with the wisdom of the mind and body.

Before I share these two acute stress patterns, I feel it is helpful to mention that I am not coming from a traditional background in psychology. I am a holistic health coach specializing in the intricate mindbody stress connection. Although I did initially explore a concentration in psychology, I sensed it was not the right angle of study for me (at least not twenty years ago when there was much less emphasis on understanding the wisdom of the body and the importance of working in harmony with its intelligence). I appreciate how this field of study has continued to evolve over the years, and I have great respect for psychologists, social workers, and therapists for the extraordinary work they do. I have often referred clients in their direction when it felt like coaching was not the right fit for them. But as for me personally, where I lit up in my studies was in philosophy. I loved how my professors rigorously challenged me to expand my capacity of how well I could question, contemplate, and observe a subject. As a foundational starting point, we questioned everything, including consciousness and reality itself. Societal beliefs were put under the microscope, and no topic was ever viewed as an absolute truth; instead, each was an exercise designed to open up our minds and push our limits to ask difficult questions and discover new angles of possibilities.

Looking back on the greater arc of my life, I recognize the higher purpose of why my intuition led me down a nontraditional path. It wasn't easy forging a new trail with other mindbody health pioneers whose focus was to honor and work with the intelligence of the body. That said, it has been worth the effort because it seems clear that now more than ever, we need a wide variety of approaches to try and solve the staggering number of people worldwide who are suffering with mental and emotional stress. I hope my angle of research can contribute to the collective effort as we all work together to tackle the far-reaching global increase in mental health challenges, as well as chronic stress-related diseases like diabetes, heart disease, autoimmune conditions, etc.

That was an important side note, but one key reason I felt called to mention that I chose to take a nontraditional path into the healing arts is because these two stress patterns that I am about to share with you are not new to psychology, and they are not rocket science. You've heard of them before, but most likely not from the angle we'll be exploring them in *Anchoring into Grace*, so please keep an open mind as we dive in.

With that said—after working with such a diverse group of individuals from around the world and hearing what they feared the most and what their greatest pains were—here are the two most common stress patterns that kept showing up again and again with my clients (some individuals experienced both stress patterns, while others experienced only one):

1. Growing up, these individuals experienced an unstable or unpredictable environment.

On any given day, they weren't sure if it was going to be a good day or a bad day when they got home, such as navigating a parent who was intimidating, emotionally unpredictable, in a bad mood, or who had a scary temper. Over time, this led them to walk on eggshells and not feel entirely safe and secure deep down. If they felt safe and secure growing up at home, these individuals may have been bullied at school or experienced an unexpected, painful event that was beyond their control, such as their parents getting divorced or experiencing the death of a loved one. Each of these different life experiences fostered an unconscious habit of anticipating or bracing for something bad to happen. (Later in adult life, these were typically unconscious fears that often resulted in an individual feeling overly tense, anxious, or sensitive to the moods and emotions of other people just going about his or her normal day.)

2. These individuals grew up with a highly critical or emotionally unavailable parent.

These individuals had a parent who put incredibly high expectations on them, and in turn, the love they received was often experienced as conditional. If they did well and did things correctly—they felt loved. If they did not meet a parent's high expectations—they did not feel unconditionally loved. Over time, this led to an internal pressure of feeling like they couldn't make a mistake and that they had to do everything right to avoid being a disappointment or to avoid being criticized. If they did not experience high levels of criticism at home, they may have been bullied at school, had two or more siblings (whom they rivaled with for their parents' love and attention), or they had a parent who was not around very much due to work, was emotionally unavailable, manipulative, or had abandoned them. (All of these stressful dynamics over a period of years, often led individuals to battle a nagging sense of emptiness and/or a need to overwork themselves to achieve the best results in order to feel valuable, receive approval, or to be loved, etc.)

Take a nice deep breath in …

And exhale.

As a loving reminder, it is wise to approach this material with an empowered mindset. A mindset where you have had enough pain and frustration and you are READY to understand the underlying problem so that you can do something about it. Or as Martin Luther King, Jr. once powerfully said:

> *"As my sufferings mounted, I soon realized that there were two ways that I could respond to my situation: either to react with bitterness or seek to transform that suffering into a creative force. I decided to follow the latter course."*

If you did not relate to either of the two stress patterns above (or you think they are too generalized for you), don't worry — that's okay, as these were not the surface complaints my clients came to work with me on.

Perhaps you can better relate to one or more of these daily challenges:

- Feeling overworked while trying to juggle all of your responsibilities (with the added pressure of feeling that you can't let one ball drop or make a mistake).
- Feeling anxious on a regular basis and worrying that something bad might happen at work, with your kids, etc.
- Feeling exhausted trying to hold it all together, but

still feeling like you are falling short or disappointing someone.

- Feeling frozen or chronically worrying about finances (even if you have enough to pay the bills).
- Being extra-sensitive to the moods and emotions of people around you and feeling like you're walking on eggshells in order to avoid setting off a disagreement.
- Being sick and tired of not being treated well by your partner or having weekly arguments with him or her.
- Needing outer validation or recognition from others.
- Being highly sensitive when people are mad at you, disappointed in you, or critical of you.
- Feeling like you need to get everything done on your massive to-do list and that there is never enough time.
- Waking up in the middle of the night in a panic or having difficulty sleeping.
- Feeling burnt-out, overwhelmed, anxious, disconnected, or depressed.
- Running on fumes and feeling numb, disconnected, and unhappy.
- Needing to decompress with a drink, comfort foods, or hours of TV in order to switch your mind off and relax.

In the next chapter, I will give you a full list of 24 examples related to these two stress patterns to help you better gauge which ones might have impacted you while growing up.

For our purposes in this chapter—and in order to understand why your survival stress response is being triggered throughout the day by non-life-threatening situations—we first need to look at these stress patterns more closely.

Over time, what became evident to me was that regardless of how different my clients' life experiences were, deep down they were experiencing either current stress or past resentment around these two primary concerns: they did not feel loved, seen, valued, or respected in their relationships; and/or they did not feel adequately safe, stable, or secure, and they were bracing for the other shoe to drop or for something bad to happen.

At the heart of their tears ... this is what came through.

At the core of their boiling anger and overwhelming fears ... this is what came through.

I didn't find anything underneath it.

What became apparent over time is that the need to feel safe and the need to feel loved are:

Survival Needs

In any given moment, if we do not feel safe and secure deep down—this can activate our survival stress response.

If we do not feel like we belong, if we do not feel loved, respected, seen, or valued—this can activate our fight, flight, freeze response.

In essence, these two needs are non-negotiable—they must be met moment by moment—in order for us to be able to fully relax and feel at ease inside ourselves.

For instance, if you are experiencing a challenge (big or small) and you perceive that your needs to feel loved and/or safe are not being met, you may experience a low to high-level stress response.

A low-level stress response can look something like:

- Feeling anxious or being on edge but not knowing why.
- Feeling overly sensitive to other people's moods or taking things personally.
- Feeling a level of tension or unease as a constant companion as you go about your day.
- Excessively doubting yourself or lacking confidence.
- Feeling frustrated, impatient, and reactive when things don't go your way.
- Being moody, short, mean, or irritable.
- Numbing out with food, drinking, etc.

(All of the above are quite common, so I'm not suggesting you will never feel stress again. But rather, what I am suggesting is that it is possible to decrease your levels of everyday unease and increase your ability to experience more ease, peace, and pleasure in your life.)

A high-level stress response can look something like:

- Feeling extremely anxious and being unable to calm your mind and body down.
- Feeling frozen or overwhelmed and being unable to take action or to think clearly.
- Experiencing panic attacks.
- Boiling over in anger or shouting in an argument.
- Repressing anger and passive-aggressively refusing to communicate.
- Needing to escape and being unable to handle a situation or circumstance altogether.

Take a nice deep breath in …

And exhale.

I want you to take heart in knowing *that you are uneasy for a reason*. When you understand the deeper functioning of your survival program, you will be able to understand why you are holding on so tightly just going about your normal day. In consciously understanding this level within yourself, you will be able to address the root problem, self-heal, and change your life in beautiful and profound ways. So please stick with me on this because we have another KEY component to investigate.

To continue peeling away the layers and understand why you're defaulting into stress and tension just going about your normal day, the next question we need to ask is:

> *Why is our survival mode chronically being triggered throughout the day when, by and large as adults, we have food, clothing, shelter, and people in our lives who love us?*

A primary reason that our survival needs to feel safe and loved are STILL so raw for us as adults is that—despite our many differences and unique childhood experiences—we all share one thing in common:

> *We were all once vulnerable children who were dependent on our parents or guardians for the first 15-20 years of our lives—and after two decades of learning to navigate the world from this dependent, vulnerable position—our nervous system developed an engrained habit of being overly sensitive to circumstances happening around us.*

To help you understand the true depth of what I'm presenting, I'd like you to pull back and think about it from this perspective …

From the moment you took your first breath, you were a completely helpless newborn, 100% dependent on your parents or guardians to survive. Hour by hour, if you needed to be fed, kept warm, nurtured, loved, changed, protected, and comforted, you were dependent upon someone outside of yourself to take care of you, to help you feel better, and to make sure your needs were being met. You couldn't take care of yourself on your own. You wouldn't have survived.

In addition, compared to other species, humans remain vulnerable and dependent for a much greater length of time. Take, for example, a baby giraffe that abruptly drops five feet onto the ground when it is born. Within a matter of hours, this baby must coordinate its long, awkward legs to be able to run on its first day of life. In comparison, the average age for humans to begin walking is twelve months.

However, what is more important beyond our acute dependency during the first few years of our lives, is our EXTENDED DEPENDENCY, which lasts well into our late teens and early twenties, as we continue to stay heavily reliant upon our parents or guardians to provide us with food, clothing, shelter, attention, and love.

With this in mind, it impresses upon us to ask ourselves these questions:

> How did being heavily dependent on others during the first 15-20 years of my life— influence how I handle stress as an adult when I don't feel like my needs are being met?

> When my needs to feel safe and/or loved weren't adequately or consistently met as a child—what did I do to try and get my needs met?

In order to answer these questions, we must explore **evolutionary dependency ...**

What is evolutionary dependency?

Evolutionary dependency focuses predominantly on these four components:

- It explores how you were mentally, emotionally, and physically dependent on others to get your survival needs to feel safe and loved adequately met during the first 15-20 years of your life.

- It equally observes the ways you tried to get your needs met when you did not feel safe, secure, loved, or seen during your childhood, as well as the strengths you developed in order to try to improve your situation to get your needs met.

- It also addresses how to consciously bring your strengths into balance so as not to unconsciously use them excessively or in ways that are counterproductive for you as an adult, which can fuel burnout, conflicts in relationships, and chronic stress.

- Lastly, it explores how to get your survival needs met on a higher, more reliable level so that you can be strong and calm in the world (even if there is a great deal of stress happening around you).

If you are familiar with the topic of codependency, you might be wondering if it is similar to evolutionary dependency—or if you are not familiar with the subject of codependency—you might feel a bit out of the loop with these two new terms being introduced! For both of these reasons, I want to briefly look at codependency and evolutionary dependency and what differentiates them. I will also introduce the importance of addressing our unconscious, habitual dependency on others (as this dependency is directly linked to fueling our overactive survival stress response and why we need a clear, logical, and grounded solution to counter this tendency).

To begin, what differentiates evolutionary dependency and codependency is the angle of study and focus.

Codependency is based on identifying behaviors in human relationships that are viewed as unhealthy and dysfunctional, with individuals attempting to get their needs primarily met from someone outside of themselves. The origin of this toxic, unhealthy behavior is believed to stem from a dysfunctional childhood. One problem with viewing something solely from a dysfunctional perspective is that it views symptoms as being wrong, unhealthy, or meaningless. Not only does this make codependency difficult to solve and truly heal from, but it can also weigh an individual down with tremendous shame, guilt, confusion, and resentment, as well as unnecessarily chain a person to the past.

Evolutionary dependency, on the other hand, focuses on childhood stress from an evolutionary biological, mental, emotional, and spiritual point of view that honors the wisdom within you and your drive to survive. **From this vantage point, we ask different questions and from here you can begin to discover that evolutionary dependency is not a dysfunction—nor is it a weakness in you**. Instead, it is a highly advanced survival strategy that helped you to navigate your childhood and to get your needs met when you were vulnerable, dependent, and disempowered in the adult-child dynamic.

> (This angle of my research eventually led me to create a new term to describe codependency—as *evolutionary dependency*—as it seemed more accurate from a mindbody, evolutionary point of view when we look at children's adaptability and positive intent on finding empowering ways to get their needs met.)

This will not be another book on codependency, as many other valuable books have been written on this subject, that in addition, address crucial topics that I will not be touching on here. **Instead,** *Anchoring into Grace* **will offer a complementary perspective that will focus on investigating the higher intention and biological purpose within the** *symptoms of codependency*.

For example:

WHY is someone overly sensitive to the moods and emotions of other people?
WHY is someone overly anxious, a people pleaser, or conflict avoidant?
WHY is someone controlling, judgmental, or overly critical?
WHY is someone a perfectionist or Type A?
WHY are people overworking themselves in order to seek outer validation or striving for social status and recognition at the cost of their own happiness?
WHY are people compelled to make everyone happy even at the cost of their own well-being?

These are common symptoms of codependency. But what is

really fueling all of this and how can we address these challenges with a clear, logical, and empowering solution?

Evolutionary dependency answers these questions while simultaneously removing the shame or guilt that can often accompany these codependent behaviors. When you understand WHY you are doing something and learn to appreciate the higher wisdom and positive intention fueling your actions, you will be able to bring these behaviors within you into balance with greater ease. After I introduce my clients to the concepts of evolutionary dependency in their first session, many of my clients tear up and *feel* their intrinsic worth in a way they hadn't been able to tap into for years.

In the next chapter, I will introduce 24 examples to help you discern which stress patterns might have impacted you while you were growing up. But before we move on, I want to briefly explain how your subconscious mind can play a crucial role in your healing. Your subconscious mind can either help you to reverse your overactive survival stress response, or it can keep you stuck in a state of perpetual stress.

Since we are working with powerful, instinctive, survival forces within you, it is important to understand that evolutionary dependency is inseparable from your body's survival program—and that your survival program is inseparable from your subconscious mind. Your subconscious mind is powerful; in fact, scientists have documented that your subconscious mind is able to process millions of pieces of information per second, compared to your conscious mind, which processes a far more limited amount. A study referenced in Dr. Bruce Lipton's book, *Biology of Belief*, demonstrates the different capacities of these two levels of your mind beautifully:

"If a ball comes near your eye, the slower conscious mind may not have time to be aware of the threatening projectile. Yet the subconscious mind, which processes some 20,000,000 environmental stimuli per second v. 40 environmental stimuli interpreted by the conscious mind in the same second, will cause the eye to blink. The subconscious mind, the most powerful information processor known, specifically observes both the surrounding world and the body's internal awareness, reads the environmental cues, and immediately engages previously acquired (learned) behaviors—all without the help, supervision, or even awareness of the conscious mind." (136).

Referencing the impressive power of your subconscious mind is by no means minimizing the ability of your conscious mind. On the contrary, your conscious mind is extremely powerful, and it is crucial for you to harness the greater potential of your conscious mind in your healing journey. But in the same breath, you'll want to equally learn how to get your subconscious mind on board with your desire to be more calm and at ease as you go about your daily life.

The *Anchoring into Grace Method*™ within this book is specifically designed to work in harmony with your subconscious mind, your survival program, and with the greater wisdom of life within you. Why? Because there is an unfathomable level of intelligence, organization, and function transpiring within you at every moment to keep you alive. Your body has over 50 trillion human cells that build into different tissues and organ systems which allow you the gift of being able to breathe, perceive, see, touch, smell, taste, live, love, be, and do in the world.

For instance:

- How does your body transform wavelengths of light into your ability to see color, shapes, and spatial dimensions?
- How are you able to think, feel, and speak?
- How does your body digest food, breathe oxygen, and circulate life-giving nutrients to each one of your 50 trillion cells?
- How do you turn sound waves into cognitive communication? If someone yells at you to run, how do you digest this sound, translate it into meaning, and then switch into a survival stress response and run like crazy?
- How does your body heal a broken bone or wound?
- How does your body reproduce the next generation of life?
- What organizes the coherent function of your brain that is made up of over 100 billion neurons? How do these brain cells relay messages and communicate to one another through synapses?

"In a human, there are more than 125 trillion synapses just in the cerebral cortex alone. That is roughly equal to the number of stars in 1,500 Milky Way galaxies."

- Dr. Steven Smith

The truth is, there is an incomprehensible level of intelligence within you—and it behooves you to work in harmony with this intelligence and not against it. Your body is not making a mistake. You are anxious, tense, controlling, critical, irritable, and unable to relax for a reason. You want to understand what the reason is so that you can self-heal from the inside out.

If you try and fight against your body's subconscious mind and survival program, if you don't understand or respect their higher intelligence and purpose, then trying to overpower these parts of yourself is the equivalent to tirelessly racing up a steep, rugged mountain that has no summit. (Or to put it another way, if there was a match between your conscious and subconscious mind—a 40 versus a 20,000,000 processing system—which part of you do you think would win in the long run?)

On the other hand, if you work in harmony *with* your body's survival program, you can change unwanted, stress-inducing habits with grace. Which is why I set out to research codependency and the overactive survival stress response from a biological, evolutionary point of view. It is directly through understanding the higher purpose and intelligence within your stress response that you can collaborate *with* your body in order to feel more calm and peaceful—even amidst a hectic, chaotic world.

Before I move on from the topic of codependency, I want to emphasize that I am not seeking to minimize the invaluable research, expertise, or literature on codependency—as this is a crucial and complex area of study—and I wouldn't be where I am today in my own healing without the wisdom shared by so many before me. I have great appreciation for those who have had the patience, tenacity, and wisdom to tackle this illusive subject—as it can be counterintuitive at the best of times—and it is equally tied to some of humanity's greatest suffering. Additionally, I will be looking at some levels of codependency within this book, but certainly not all of them. My goal in *Anchoring into Grace* is to contribute to the conversation rather than take anything away from what others have generously shared.

Great job on getting through this chapter. We've covered quite a bit!

Please know that the concepts I've introduced will become more clear, digestible, and graspable as we move along. I'll round it off by saying that through the *Anchoring into Grace Method* within this book, you can discover that **hidden within your childhood stress and dependency is a great deal to teach you about yourself, as well as an invitation for you to heal on the deepest level of who you are**. I encourage you to keep this empowered perspective and lightness in mind because if you stick with the process and finish this book, you can be beautifully rewarded.

To summarize:

We all have two basic survival needs: the need to feel safe and the need to feel loved. If we perceive that these needs are not being met at any given moment, this can trigger a low to high-level stress response. In addition, growing up, we were dependent on others to get our survival needs met, and when these needs were not adequately or consistently met, it meant that we had to do something to improve our situation to get these needs met. What we did to get our survival needs met simultaneously helped us to develop some of our greatest strengths (as you'll soon learn more about in the coming chapters).

With that said, in order to honor the wisdom within you and begin to understand your deepest survival needs and your greatest strengths, the first step in the *Anchoring into Grace Method* is to identify:

What is my Achilles' heel survival need?

What is triggering my fight, flight, freeze response while I'm just going about my normal day-to-day life?

When you understand your triggers, you can bring logic to the intensity of your emotions and begin to take your power back …

"A challenge is a dragon with a gift in its mouth.
Tame the dragon and the gift is yours."

~ Noela N. Evans

3

What is my Achilles' heel survival need?
What is triggering my fight, flight,
freeze response whileI'm just going
about my normal day-to-day life?

Give yourself a moment and pause.

Take a nice deep breath in.

And exhale …

This book is about grace.

This book is about love.

This book is about reclaiming your power, connecting to your inner healer, and learning how it is possible to anchor into peace even when chaos is going on around you.

First, you want to identify a root problem, so that you can focus on a solution.

It is important that you understand what is triggering you, so that you can understand your triggers from a place of logic. From there, you can begin to change your default protective response and pull back on over-reacting in order to create new responses that are grounded in love, empowerment, and wisdom.

If you have reflected on your childhood or done therapy around it, you may have negativity, resentment, and blame when you think about your parents. But in this book I am going to offer a different perspective because you can't change that you were vulnerable and dependent growing up. You can't change stressful things that happened to you in your childhood or how your parents treated you.

That is not where your power lies.

Your power lies in going deeper and discovering that inherent within your childhood dependency was equally what birthed many of your greatest strengths (and was even an activator of your highest values and life's purpose)—and in order to self-heal and change your life for the better—you need to understand the first twenty years of your life from the level of love, purpose, and wisdom.

This is where your power lies.

Not in your negative or painful stories about the past, but in consciously understanding how **your adversity brought out the best in you**.

When you truly get this, it will help you to stop working against yourself, as well as how to experience new levels of peace, joy, and meaning in your life—all of which are essential ingredients to self-heal and change your life.

So stick with me as we dive into Step 1 in the *Anchoring into Grace Method*, where I will share a list of stressful childhood examples from my clients, so you can better gauge which stress patterns might be triggering you throughout the day.

Before you read through the examples please do these five things:

1. Since you are reading these childhood examples instead of hearing them directly from me in a coaching session, I recommend reading through them from a place of **lightness** and **curiosity**. Many of my clients experience relief in hearing the list and realizing they are not alone; however, if at any time you get triggered reading through the examples, know that you are in control and you have the power to stop anytime you want. You have the choice to read through the list another time with a friend, skip to the next section, book a session with me or another mental health care provider. Just know you are in control.

2. **Please read the childhood examples in reference to yourself first.** Do not get distracted and focus on the examples based on your partner's childhood. This is a very common thing to do, but I assure you, it's not your partner you need to focus on right now, so please read through the list reflecting on the examples for yourself first.

3. If you are a parent, I also need you to focus on yourself right now. You can think about this from a mother/father role shortly and how your behaviors or partner's behaviors might be impacting your kids—but if you don't put your oxygen mask on first and get 100% clear on how stressful things in **your** childhood impacted **you** and are **still** impacting you—then you won't actually be helping your kids. Guilt and worry aren't going to make things better for your children, so do this deeper work and focus on being conscious of what is going on inside yourself—as that will help your kids. (Fortunately, you'll soon learn in the following chapters that many of your greatest strengths directly stemmed from the adversity

you experienced growing up, and this equally holds true for your children.)

4. If you're the type of person who doesn't like "dredging up the past," please remember that **we're investigating your past in order to understand your present** and why your mental and emotional triggers are stuck in a repeating loop. In order to solve the problems you're currently experiencing—be it weekly conflicts with your partner, being overly hard on yourself, or chronic stress-related health problems, etc.—you'll want to solve the problems at their roots, as this is what opens the door for grace to come into your life.

5. **Disclaimer: This is not a diagnosis.** This exercise is for education purposes only.

Okay, great. With that all said, let's get started!

Anchoring into Grace Method™

Step 1: What survival need is triggering your flight, fight, freeze response?

Directions:

1. Put a check next to any of the examples you relate with as being similar to experiences you had in your own childhood.

2. Tally your totals at the bottom.

3. Give yourself 5-10 minutes to complete this exercise.

Sensitive Stress Triggers Connected to Safety, Security, and Stability

In your childhood you experienced one or more of the following:	
One or both of your parents had a temper and you sometimes walked on eggshells around him or her and tried to be on your best behavior to avoid getting in trouble.	
Your parents did not verbally argue or shout, but they were passive-aggressive with each other. There were times when they wouldn't talk to one another (or to you) for days, weeks, or even longer and the tension was palpable.	
A family member was an alcoholic or struggled with some type of addiction, which fueled a chaotic, unpredictable household. Each day you didn't know if it was going to be a good day or a bad day, and there were often emotional outbursts and drama each week with unpredictable highs and lows.	
Growing up you moved one or more times and it was stressful being uprooted from an environment you knew; or you started a new school and fitting into a new social group was stressful for you.	
You feel strongly that your parents did the best they could. You rarely think about the past, and sure, maybe one of your parents yelled and had a bit of a temper, but it wasn't a big deal to you.	
A loved one passed away from a long-term illness or died unexpectedly.	
Your parents divorced.	
Growing up you were bullied at school and felt disliked or afraid of some of your peers.	
You grew up in a rough neighborhood and did not always feel safe outside your home.	
You were verbally, emotionally, physically, or sexually abused.	
You grew up in a highly religious family or school and there was tremendous pressure on you to follow strict religious teachings. If you broke the rules or did something bad, you feared God wouldn't love you, and you'd be faced with existential punishment, bad karma, etc.	
Growing up you experienced discrimination and bigotry due to race; gender; social or economic status; religious beliefs and/or sexual orientation.	
Total check marks:	

Sensitive Stress Triggers Connected to Not Feeling Unconditionally Loved

In your childhood you experienced one or more of the following:	
You grew up with a highly critical parent who had unrealistic expectations on you. You did your absolute best in everything, but still got looks of disappointment anytime you fell short of his or her expectations. In some ways, it made you feel like you had to be perfect and anything less was unacceptable.	
One or both of your parents were conditional in their love. If you did well, you felt loved and got positive attention or praise. If you didn't do well, you didn't get positive attention and you didn't feel good enough to be loved unconditionally.	
One or both of your parents worked long hours and sometimes you felt they cared more about their careers than you. They often came home late and weren't present and connected with you, and deep down, you wanted more of their love, connection, and attention.	
You feel strongly that your parents did the best they could raising you. You rarely think about the past, and sure, maybe they had high expectations, and you didn't want to disappoint them, but it wasn't a big deal to you. You love your parents very much and are very protective of your family.	
You grew up with two or more siblings and you didn't always get the amount of connection, love, and attention from your parents that you wanted. You may have been a bit competitive or jealous with your siblings.	
You were very religious growing up and you feared sinning, making mistakes, and not being loved by God.	
As a kid, you remember everything going well and being happy when out of the blue one or both of your parents emotionally pulled away from you, shut down, became sick, or got depressed. During this period, as they were working through their pain or health problems (which you could feel but you didn't know what it was about), they stopped connecting with you and you felt alone and sensed that their emotional absence had something to do with you. You didn't know what was going on or why they stopped connecting with you, and deep down you wondered if they had pulled away because you yourself weren't good enough or because you were unlovable.	

One or both of your parents never told you they loved you and didn't hug you often - if at all. You noticed this and wished that they would.	
You were bullied in school and did not feel accepted for who you were.	
Your parents got divorced and one or both of your parents didn't make much time for you, started a new family, or you felt they put his or her new partner and kids ahead of you.	
You felt like the black sheep of the family. One of your siblings seemed to do everything right and you felt like a disappointment.	
Growing up you experienced discrimination and bigotry due to race; gender; social or economic status; religious beliefs and/or sexual orientation.	
Total check marks:	

Okay take a nice deep breath in …

And exhale …

Notice if you are holding any tension in your stomach, jaw, or neck.

Gently shake your head, torso, and arms and lovingly tell your body:

*"In this moment I am okay. In this moment I am safe.
In this moment I am taking my power back."*

You can move, get a drink of water, and walk around a bit if that feels good too.

My purpose in giving you these childhood examples is not to weigh you down, but to help you **reclaim the inner peace that is available to you at all times and is your birth right**.

Okay, let's complete Step 1:

1. After reading through the examples and tallying up the totals, which category had the most checkmarks?
(Circle the answer below)

Safety & Security   **Love & Connection**   **Equal**

Upon reflection, as you go about your day-to-day adult life, which survival need might be an area of sensitivity for you? Which survival need might be triggering your survival stress response in non-life-threatening situations?

- Do you feel somewhat sensitive or protective around not feeling entirely safe, stable, or secure deep down?
- Do you feel somewhat sensitive or protective around not feeling adequately loved, seen, respected, liked, or appreciated deep down?
- Is it a combination of both? If so, is one trigger slightly more sensitive?

   (If you could not relate with any of the examples given up above, don't worry. The following two questions can help you to isolate what might be triggering your survival stress response throughout the day.)

2. Write down two current life challenges that are causing you stress.

For example, what challenges are you currently experiencing on a regular basis that prompted you to buy this book? (Consider daily stressors at work, with your partner, finances, health, kids, etc.)

Stress 1:

Stress 2:

3. Now that you've isolated a couple of your present-day life challenges—what are these challenges triggering in you deep down?

Below the surface of your challenges, do you feel like you are not being adequately loved, respected, accepted, understood, valued, or appreciated? Alternatively, are you minimizing your own value or being overly hard on yourself? Or do you feel like within your challenges your safety and security are not as stable as you would like them to be?

Based on the examples of the life challenges you listed above, circle which survival need is being triggered within that stress:

Stress 1

   Not adequately: Loved/Respected   Safe/Secure   Both

Stress 2:

   Not adequately: Loved/Respected   Safe/Secure   Both

For example, let's say you're worried about losing your job. Would you feel more stress around feeling like a failure, caring what other people think, losing your status, not being seen and respected—or would you be more concerned about your financial instability and loss of security? It can be *both*, but usually there is one that has a *bigger sensitivity*.

Keep in mind — it is not what happens to you — it is how you perceive what happens to you. How you perceive something gives you direct insight into your Achilles' heel trigger.

4. Take a deep breath in …

And exhale.

If you are feeling any heavy emotions or angst inside yourself — know that this is not a bad thing — *it is the opposite actually*. In this moment, you are taking your power back and shining the light of your awareness on what is calling out for your attention, compassion, and understanding. On the surface, your challenges can be engulfed in negative emotions, but below this, your challenges can equally be understood as catalysts for your freedom and the opportunity to heal on the deepest level of who you are. In the next chapter we are going to explore what strengths arose within you directly out of your childhood adversity, and later in the book, we will discover how these gifts have supported you in invaluable ways throughout your life. Through this process of transforming your pain into a higher purpose, you can authentically begin to increase your confidence and self-worth, as well as strengthen your ability to connect to an ocean of peace that is always available to you. Or as Janet Baird shared when reflecting on the deeper healing that is available within suffering:

> *"A lotus sprouts at the bottom of a pond in the middle of the mud and murky water. It struggles and fights its way to the top reaching toward the light. When it finally reaches the surface it blooms beautiful and pure, untouched by all the mud it had been in."*

Wonderful job on completing Step 1.

To summarize:

In this chapter, you identified what survival needs were not adequately or consistently met for you during your childhood. Understanding this can help you to better gauge why your survival stress response is being triggered throughout the day by non-life-threatening situations. In the next chapter, you will investigate what strengths you developed in response to the adversity you experienced while growing up, and in so doing, you will be able to value yourself in ways you may have minimized yourself up until now.

To honor the wisdom within you, the next set of questions we must ask is:

> *How did it impact me when my two survival needs to feel safe and loved weren't adequately or consistently met during my childhood?*

> *What did I do to try and improve my situation to get my needs met?*

Let's dive into those two important questions in the next chapter.

Section Two:
The Discovery

In this section you will identify your greatest strengths, understand where they originated from, and learn how to use your strengths in balanced, healthy ways so that you don't unknowingly work against yourself trying to do the impossible and unwittingly be stuck in a repeating loop of chronic stress.

4

How did it impact me when my two survival needs to feel safe and loved weren't adequately or consistently met during my childhood?

What did I do to try and improve my situation to get my needs met?

These are life-changing questions.

When you take the time to investigate and answer them, you will understand why you're tense just going about your normal day and why it can be difficult to relax without the nagging pressure of your responsibilities constantly creeping in.

To begin answering these questions, first we must acknowledge that while you were growing up, you were disempowered in the adult-child relationship and you didn't get to have the ultimate say in how calm, loving, or peaceful your home environment was. If your parents were having another scary argument, or you were constantly being criticized and felt like nothing you did was ever good enough, at five or ten years old you couldn't say: "You know what? I've had enough of this! I'm moving out and getting my own place. This isn't healthy for me. I don't like how I am being treated. I'm outta here!"

How would you have paid for rent, food, or the bills? What landlord would have rented to a kid? (If you did run away, you might have stayed equally vulnerable.) In consequence, you were disempowered in the adult-child dynamic for almost the first two decades of your life; however, that didn't mean you were *entirely powerless* …

So where was *your* power?

Growing up you couldn't completely change your living situation, **but you did have the ability to *improve* it as best you could. Therefore, your power existed in how you could** *influence your environment.*

In essence, if your needs weren't being adequately met, it meant that you had to do something to get your needs met, and it is directly out of how you tried to improve your environment that you began (out of necessity) to develop some of your greatest strengths. And these strengths did not just aid you well in childhood, they have continued to support you in invaluable ways throughout your adult life as well.

Why am I confident some of your greatest strengths are directly connected to not having your survival needs met in your childhood?

After years of working with people from many walks of life, I have observed another commonality between us. I've discovered that each of my clients found wise, strategic, and innovative ways to positively influence and improve their childhood environment. In addition, we investigated how these strengths aided them throughout the decades of their adult lives, and the insights were always humbling and profound.

In taking the time to investigate what you did to improve your well-being and security growing up, you can open the door to being more confident in who you are on a deep, authentic level.

Let's look at several concrete examples to help you get a clear idea of exactly what I mean.

If your family struggled financially while you were growing up and you felt your parents' fears of not knowing how they were going to make ends meet and you took on their fears as well—what might you have done to help create more safety and security for yourself and for your family?

Perhaps you developed innovative abilities as a problem solver ...

If there was constant stress around money, you could have brainstormed ways to make life easier for your parents by taking care of your siblings to help take the pressure off them, or you could have started your own business by babysitting or mowing lawns. If you were constantly exposed to financial strain, it could have ignited a desire in you to be financially empowered, and in response, you may have developed a clear strategy as to how you could change your own financial trajectory in the future. Perhaps you did this by being a disciplined student, getting a scholarship, being accepted into a good school, or securing a career that offered safety and stability for you.

> Developing the skills of an adept problem solver during the first twenty years of your life can set you up to succeed for the next eighty years. There is very little a person can't accomplish if one has a can-do attitude, knowing that within every problem is an opportunity and a solution.

What if you had a parent who was anxious or depressed?

What could you have done to make your parent feel better, and in turn, get more love and connection from him or her?

You could have developed strengths as a nurturer or a healer …

If one or both of your parents were anxious or sad, you could have developed abilities to nurture and comfort them. If you could get your parents to feel better and be happy, then you could feel their love in your direction and you could feel better too.

> Having natural healing abilities could have fostered your skills of intuition, empathy, connecting with healing energy that is beyond logic, and being a heart-centered person. All of these skills that were fostered and strengthened in you during the first twenty years could help you to become a great health care provider, friend, or parent for the rest of your life.

What if you had a parent who was highly critical? What could you have done to avoid criticism and to feel loved?

You could have developed skills as a perfectionist and become a hard worker …

Having a highly critical parent could have challenged you to get in touch with your true potential and empowered your skills for being determined, self-disciplined, focused, and goal-oriented. Having these abilities could have helped you get exceptional grades, get into a great school, meet influential people along your journey who synchronistically opened doors for you, and helped lead you toward a successful career.

> Perhaps being a perfectionist and having a strong work ethic helped you to be financially empowered

as an adult, which allowed you to be a good provider for your family, travel around the world, and have amazing adventures you wouldn't otherwise have been able to have if you weren't as financially successful.

What if your parents fought on a regular basis? What could you have done to calm the environment and feel safer?

You could have developed the strengths of being a mediator or a peacemaker ...

If your parents were arguing or if there was some type of passive-aggressive conflict going on, you could have been a mediator diffusing the situation by helping your family members to better communicate with each other, understand everyone's points of view, and resolve the conflict.

> Developing the skills as a mediator or peacemaker during the first twenty years of your life could support you in invaluable ways for the next eighty years of your life. By being able to understand everyone's point of view—you could use this ability to experience healthier communication, more love, trust, and understanding in your personal relationships—as well as how to more effectively resolve conflicts at work.

Or you could have done the opposite:

You could have become an escapist ...

Your strategy could have been to try to avoid the drama and conflict altogether by going to your friend's house, high-tailing it to your room, spending time in nature, staying late at school, diving into sports or your studies, partying with your friends, or devoting yourself to the arts. In moving away from conflict and toward something that made you feel better, this could have helped you to develop close friendships or to develop specialized skills in sports, arts, or the sciences.

> We might not see an escapist as a strength on the surface, but if we peer a bit deeper, we can discover that married with this trait is often an individual who doesn't let life pass him or her by, and he or she is often adventurous, courageous, outgoing, friendly, a world traveler, or gifted in the arts or sciences.

What if you had a parent who had a bad temper? What could you have done to decrease your chances of getting in trouble? How could you have calmed the situation down in order to feel more safe and secure?

You could have developed a sharp sense of humor …

If you had a parent who was chronically in a bad mood, you could have been witty and told jokes to get him or her to lighten up, forget about what they were stewing at, and be less aggressive toward you and the rest of your family. Humor is a great skill with the ability to completely change the environment and make everyone feel safer and more relaxed, as well as to have love and appreciation sent your way.

> Later in life, having a good sense of humor is a wonderful asset to have. Making people laugh can be an invaluable strength to use in your career, as well as a gift that brings light-heartedness to your personal relationships. For some, having a gifted sense of humor can even lead to a full-time career as an actor,

comedian, or an entertainer bringing joy and laughter to the masses.

Now perhaps you are thinking: "I should not have had to do any of that. My parents were the adults and they should have made sure my needs were being met at all times."

To which my response is…

In chapter six, you are going to do an exercise that opens up your mind to not only own your strengths, but to see how they have served you in meaningful ways throughout your life. When you do this, and you take the time to look at the greater arc of your life in terms of decades and understand how your strengths rippled throughout your life in meaningful ways, instead of feeling resentment, it is much more likely that you will feel empowered. (Possibly even grateful if you let yourself go deep enough.)

Secondly, last time I checked, life is not a bowl of cherries. We're not Care Bears jumping around from cloud to cloud on magical rainbows. Life in the physical dimension is filled with some pretty impressive adversity. I am currently writing *Anchoring into Grace* during a global pandemic, the Black Lives Matter movement, and under skies painted a toxic orange with air that is unbreathable at times due to the massive forest fires in the West.

Perhaps the uncomfortable truth is that kids who were overly pampered by their parents in childhood can become juvenile adults who struggle with real-life responsibilities after they leave the nest. Whereas kids who experienced adversity in childhood or didn't have life handed to them on a silver platter can be a bit more prepared, mature, confident, and resilient within themselves to handle how challenging life can actually be.

You can't change your past—but you can take the empowered position when you own the strengths that were birthed in you out of your childhood adversity. In owning your gifts, you will strengthen yourself mentally, emotionally, physically, and spiritually, as well as increase your self-awareness, self-confidence, and self-worth (all of which can help you to be better equipped to handle the beautiful and intense journey of this earthly life).

I say this with LOVE because I know you have more in you than your pain.

In *Anchoring into Grace* we are going to go higher and deeper than your pain.

Because you cannot heal at the level of your suffering.

You heal at the level of love and wisdom.

It is time to appreciate yourself, your past, and your life in ways you have not done so before.

With that said, we first need to identify your strengths and survival strategies.

Let's do that now and dive into Step 2.

Step 2: Identify Survival Strategies & Strengths

Each of the traits below helped you to get your survival needs met in childhood in some way; therefore, I have termed them as: **Survival Strategies**.

Directions:

1. Put a check next to each of the survival strategies you identify with.
2. Check all the traits you relate to currently having as an adult, as well as to those traits you had when you were younger. (More often than not, survival traits strengthen over time, which means you might identify with some of the strengths below more as an adult than you did as a child. This is normal.)
3. Some of the survival strategies you'll identify as having can appear to be in dichotomy of each other. This is okay. You are a multi-level, complex human being so this is normal. (Example: you can be **responsible** in one area of your life and an **escapist** in another.)
4. If you identify as having a strength within yourself that supports you in getting your needs met but is not listed below, please trust your intuition and add this strength to the list.
5. Give yourself 5 minutes to complete this exercise.

intuitive	controlling; critical
problem solver	fastidiously clean
responsible; disciplined; serious; hard worker	rescuer; save people from their weekly crisis
peacemaker; meditate conflicts	caretaker
empathetic	people pleaser
healing abilities	chameleon; mold self to others
wise beyond your years	patient; resilient
introverted; introspective	bit of a temper; confrontational
spiritual; religious; connected to a higher energy	passive-aggressive; avoid conflicts at all costs
driven; ambitious; resourceful; strong-willed	stuff emotions; pretend everything is okay
connect easily with others; make friends quickly	addictive behaviors (alcohol, TV, internet, drugs, sex)
perfectionist	irresponsible
organized; focused	escapist
social; fun; outgoing	manipulative; tell white lies
comedian; funny; gifted at making people laugh	charming; charm others to get what you want
adventurer; explorer	OCD tendencies
a leader	sensitive to other's opinions
protective of others	sensitive to other's emotions
confront problems directly; truth-teller	seek approval and validation from others
warrior spirit; courageous	overly hard on yourself
a rebel; rise up against the status quo	distant; shut down; pull away to protect yourself
innovative	demanding
anxious	gifted at sports
strategic; analytical; plan well for the future	gifted at writing, music, sciences, or the arts

more of the parent than the child growing up; mature	extroverted; magnanimous; big-hearted
orbit around others	sad
independent	competitive
strict rule-follower	chronic health challenges
networker	hypochondriac
good listener	kind
play small to appease others	flirtatious
workaholic	innovative thinker; visionary
good communicator	humanitarian; environmentalist
Trait not listed? Trust yourself and add it to the list:	

6. List the top 5-10 traits you identify as having, and not just traits that seem positive on the surface:

1	6
2	7
3	8
4	9
5	10

You may be thinking:

Some of these traits aren't strengths at all. In fact, they are my weaknesses and cause me a great deal of suffering. This is understandable and valid; however, when you look *below the surface*, you might be surprised by the underlying, *positive intention driving each of your unwanted behaviors*. That is why

I call these survival strategies. The majority of your survival strategies are true strengths, while others lean more towards strategies. However, when you understand the positive intention within all of your survival strategies, and make your unconscious conscious, you will more easily be able to shift unwanted behaviors within yourself (as you will soon see in the coming chapters).

To summarize:

In this chapter, you learned that when your needs to feel loved and safe weren't adequately or consistently met growing up, it meant that you had to do something to get your needs met. How you sought to positively influence and improve your well-being in childhood is directly connected to some of your greatest strengths. In chapter 6, you will investigate how your survival strategies have served a meaningful and beneficial purpose in your life, not only in your childhood, but through the whole of your life. Doing this exercise will help you to build your self-confidence and self-worth naturally.

In honoring the wisdom within you, the next question we want to ask in the *Anchoring into Grace Method* is:

> *How did your survival strategies support you in your childhood and in beneficial ways in your adult life?*

You are getting to the lighter part of self-healing evolutionary dependency.

Keep up the good work! You're doing great.

5

To help you get the most out of this book, let's create a wise mindset going into the next two chapters.

There is a great deal of challenge happening in the world right now. I know you are busy and I am sure you are a bit tired, so before we dive into the next two chapters, I want to give you options. First, know that you do not need to do Steps 3 and 4 in the next two chapters perfectly. Simply understanding the concepts will go a long way in helping you grasp how to increase your ability to feel more calm and energized as you go about your daily life.

Second, if you are exhausted and depleted, if you are at the end of your rope, if you are spinning out in overwhelm and stress, or you are desperate for a break to feel better, **then I invite you to just read through chapters 6 and 7** and forego doing the exercises until you finish reading the book.

To self-heal, you want to cultivate peace and love within you as these energies will aid you in ways no other things can. Later in the book, in chapters 8, 9, and 10 you will learn how to fill your body with greater levels of peace, and this will calm you, give you strength, help you to focus, and give you the energy you need to do the exercises in chapters 6 and 7 more effectively. So for your first time through, don't put unnecessary pressure on yourself. Healing is about progress over perfection

… and small, consistent steps are more effective than going all in, losing steam, hitting a wall, and stopping.

The good news is, there is no right way to do this.

Healing is not a straight line.

Your journey to health and well-being is about trusting and checking in with yourself and honoring what you need. This book is not about judgment. It is about working in harmony with the wisdom within you … and sometimes that means resting first to replenish your energy.

Now, if you are enjoying this material, but are finding it tricky to do the steps on your own and would like more support going through the process, I have created several options. These include a go-at-your-own-pace online course with videos to coach you through each of the steps, a live monthly group coaching program where you can ask me questions in real-time, as well as the option to work with me personally in my private 8-week coaching program. You can learn more about these different levels of support at: belladodds.com/resources

With all that said, if you are feeling good and you are ready to see how your strengths have served you in invaluable ways throughout your life, and you are ready to pull back on over-using your people pleasing tactics, perfectionism, or sensitivity to the moods and emotions of others, etc., then dive into the next two exercises.

Whatever you decide to do is right for you … just know that you can't mess this up. If you only have energy to read through chapters 6 and 7, then please do so guilt-free.

"There are a thousand ways to kneel and kiss the ground, there are a thousand ways to go home again."

~ Rumi

6

How did my survival strategies aid me in childhood and in beneficial ways throughout my adult life?

It is all too common to play small and minimize yourself, but in this chapter you are going to do the opposite.

I want you to practice SEEING YOURSELF in a beautiful light, and in so doing stand more solidly within the center of your being.

In this chapter, you are going to view your life from a higher vantage point, as though you were 500 feet above the Earth, viewing your life from the past all the way up to the present. From this higher vista, you will investigate how adversities in your childhood were actually catalysts that helped you to develop some of your most valuable traits. In addition, you will understand your childhood dependency and survival strategies—not from the perspective of right or wrong, or good or bad—**but from the level of purpose**.

For one very important reason …

As I have shared in previous chapters, when you take the time to get curious and investigate, you will see that each of your survival strategies is driven by a positive intention.

It is important that you make this positive intention conscious and that you understand the *real reason* for why you are doing something.

Why is it essential to uncover the higher intentions driving your actions?

Because if you want to change or balance an unwanted behavior such as perfectionism, people pleasing, over-working yourself, etc., it is much easier to change this behavior when you work in harmony with your survival program and you are coming from a level of gratitude that allows you to genuinely see, understand, and appreciate why you've been doing something in the first place.

Take this analogy toward changing an unwanted behavior for example:

Let's say your partner comes home one day and dumps all of his or her frustration, resentment, and disappointment on you, blames you for everything that is not working in the relationship, and then demands that you change.

How receptive do you think you'd be to this type of treatment?

Would you want to change or would you put up a protective wall and dig in?

Now, let's say your partner comes home and he or she expresses appreciation for who you are and you feel genuinely loved by your partner. Then from this healthy level of communication, your partner opens up about a challenge he or she is experiencing, not from the level of blame, but in wanting to work with you so that you two can grow stronger together as a couple.

Do you think you'd be more receptive to this level of kindness and be open to hearing what your partner had to say?

Which approach sounds easier or perhaps even beautiful?

Now let's tie this same analogy in with your relationship to your body's survival program (and your subconscious mind) and your conscious desire to be more relaxed and peaceful as you move through your day.

How do you want to have this conversation?

Do you want to seek to understand, appreciate, and acknowledge the higher purpose within your survival program and understand how it has served you throughout your life, or do you want to come from the level of control, frustration, shame, and blame?

As I mentioned in the second chapter, scientists have said that your conscious mind processes **40 stimuli per second** in comparison to your subconscious mind that processes **20 MILLION stimuli per second**. Your subconscious mind is *powerful*. It is also inseparable from your body's survival program, and one of their combined functions is to keep you alive.

What this means is that your subconscious mind is constantly watching out for you. It never leaves your side and it is looking out for your well-being 24/7.

So how then do you want to approach this inner ally?

Do you think it would be wise to show appreciation and acknowledgment for everything your survival program is doing to look out for you, or do you want to be ungrateful, learn nothing, and instead try to force this inner powerhouse to submit to your demands?

Which part of you do you think is going to win?

From years of experience, I can tell you it is *much easier* to work with the wisdom within you rather than to work against it, not to mention that it opens the door for you to have an enlightening, rewarding, and deeply healing experience.

Therefore, Step 3 is designed to help you:

1. Appreciate and understand the higher wisdom within your body's fight, flight, freeze response
2. Appreciate yourself and stop minimizing your worth and strengths
3. Begin to change your stress-inducing behaviors through the level of wisdom, purpose, and gratitude

Before we jump into Step 3, I'd like to acknowledge one of my teachers. I have been privileged to learn from exceptional mentors along my journey through the healing arts, and one who impacted the trajectory of my life in a significant way was Dr. John F. Demartini. If my path had not crossed his, I would not have learned to push myself to go farther, and uncover the higher wisdom hidden within codependency. Steps 3 and 4 were influenced by many mentors, but most significantly from what I learned studying with John. I want to thank him for all he has contributed to my life and for the healing I have personally experienced and witnessed in others using the *Demartini Method*.

The most effective way to teach you Step 3 is to share client case studies in order to make this step real and not just hypothetical.

It is essential to experience self-healing work for yourself, as only then can you *know it to be true,* but I hope these case studies will support you to open up your intuition so that you can experience seeing the higher gifts birthed out of the adversity in your own life.

To create a foundation for each case study, I will share the main challenges my clients were experiencing when they first sought out my help, as well as give a brief story of their childhood to give you a frame of reference of their underlying stress patterns. If at any time their stories are triggering for you, know that you are in control, and can skip past their brief descriptions any time you want. The main focus of these case studies will be for you to see what strengths my clients developed when their survival needs were not being adequately or consistently met in childhood, and in turn, how these traits helped my clients to improve their circumstances in getting their needs met. Additionally, you will not only discover how these strengths have served them in beneficial ways throughout their adult lives, but how they are equally connected to what my clients cherish most in their lives today.

* Although permission was given by each of my clients to share their stories in this book, names have been changed for anonymity.

Case Study #1: Sara

Why Sara sought out mindbody health coaching and wanted to work with me:

When Sara came to see me, she was anxious, overwhelmed, and exhausted. On a daily basis she struggled with high levels of guilt and worry that she was falling short as a parent, spouse, and in her career as a teacher. She was spiritual and had a strong belief that she was being supported in life, but she could only feel this peace and comfort when she was doing her spiritual practices. Sara knew that being so hard on herself as well as her routine episodes of anxiety were tied into having grown up with an alcoholic father. She was tired of having her past run her life, and Sara was ready to do something about it.

Sara's Story:
Sara grew up in a small town in Surrey, England. She had an older brother whom she was very close to and they looked out for one another. Sara's father was an alcoholic who had unpredictable mood swings and a bad temper even on his good days. Not only did he have a temper, but he was also highly critical, controlling, and made Sara and her brother do laborious, sometimes dangerous carpentry work either in his business or with home improvements. On a weekly basis, her dad released his pent-up frustration through scolding, arguing, and shouting. Sara and her mother were close, but deep down, she was resentful that her mum didn't do more to protect her and her brother. Sara longed to have a normal life like her friends at school, and she fantasied about camping and vacations she wished she could go on. When Sara was eighteen, she left home and never moved back.

What were Sara's Compromised Survival Needs?
Sara did not feel adequately safe, secure, or unconditionally loved due to her father's alcoholism, unpredictable temper, and being highly critical. Sara also did not feel her mother loved her enough because if she had, she believed her mum would have stepped up more to protect her.

What Survival Strategies did Sara develop within herself to help improve her environment and try to get her survival needs met?

sensitive to other's emotions	intuitive
independent	introverted
spiritual	responsible
empathetic	caring
protective of others	kind
mediator	wiser than her years
patient	passive-aggressive
perfectionist	hardworking

Example of Sara completing Step 3:

Select one of your childhood survival strategies to work with:
Mediator (being a peacemaker feeds into this strength as well_)_

- What need were you trying to get met by being a **mediator?**

  Love/Connection   **Safety/Security**   Both

- How did being a **mediator** help you to navigate stressful situations in your childhood?

  I understood everyone's point of view, even when my dad was being irrational. I did my best to diffuse the tension when arguments arose - sometimes it worked and sometimes it didn't, but I did my best to create a more peaceful environment - and when there was peace - I felt safer.

  I also used my kindness, empathy, and mediating skills at school. I was well-liked by many different social groups. I knew how to connect with people and was a good listener. I think being able to understand my friends and peers' *points of view made them want to spend time with me. Life was so challenging at home that my friends felt like family to me. I am still close to a few of my childhood friends to this day.*

- How did being a **mediator** help you to improve your ability to get your survival needs of feeling **safe and secure** met while you were growing up?

  Fighting made me extremely anxious and afraid while I was growing up - I hated loud arguments. My stomach would be in knots whenever the yelling started, but when I could diffuse the tension and help everyone get along better - I remember a tremendous release of pressure being lifted from me. When everyone felt okay - I felt okay too.

- How has being a **mediator** benefited you in your adult life?

  Being a good mum is incredibly important to me. I never want my kids to feel the way that I did growing up, so being a good mediator helps me in several ways as a mum. I am patient, understanding, and empathetic. I want my kids to share their voices and explain how they are feeling. If they are too emotional I can help them get in touch with how they are really feeling and create a safe space for them to communicate. As a family, we've been through challenging times, but my kids know that they can always come to me about anything. Being a good mum and having a close relationship with my children are two of the most important and fulfilling things in my life.

- How has being a **mediator** helped you in your personal relationships?

I constantly witnessed my mum being afraid to speak up for herself - I knew down to my core that I wanted to have a different type of marriage. I have disagreements with my husband like everyone else, but my ability to listen, be patient and understand where my husband is coming from helps him to soften. He is a little more quick to the trigger, but when I stay calm, he calms down too. Our ability to communicate in healthy ways has helped us grow closer and get through some tough periods over the years. He also knows I understand him on a deep level and we share a beautiful trust together. His love and our family are two of the greatest blessings in my life.

- How has being a **mediator** helped you in your career, health, and finances?

  As a teacher I can tune into the kids in my class. I can sense what's going on below the surface. I can particularly zone in on the kids who are having trouble at home. Other teachers can take their behaviors personally, but I have the patience to understand what is really going on. As a good mediator, I listen to my students, I don't just talk over them or demand that they respect me. I create a relationship based on mutual respect and trust. Students have come and confided in me about being abused and I have helped them get the resources they've needed for their safety and well-being. I love what I do and I care about changing lives - especially with the kids that need the most help.

Bonus: *Sara's New Healing Perspective*

When Sara left home, her main priority was to get as far away from her father as she could. After a year of attending university, Sara met her husband and they connected deeply. They

both wanted to have a family and give their kids a different kind of childhood than they had each experienced. They
both wanted their kids to feel safe growing up and to have
adventures they never got to experience. As a family they
went on camping trips every summer to the Lake District,
took regular trips to the ocean and family holidays around
the U.K. and Europe. They also enjoyed family night once a
week where they either played board games or had movie
nights together. Even though Sara and her husband didn't
have a lot of money, together they lived a very rich life. As a
family they went through many challenging times, but Sara
had an enormous amount of strength to endure it all. Upon
taking the time to investigate her life over a forty-year span,
Sara could see that what she was most grateful for had in
fact been simultaneously connected to the chaos and instability of her childhood—birthing within her a deep desire to
create the opposite and be a different type of parent when she
became a mum. In recognizing this, Sara took her power back
from her dad, transformed her resentment into appreciation
for her life and her strengths, and she lived her life moving
forward founded on a deeper level of self-worth and purpose.
(In self-healing all of her stress patterns on a deep level, Sara
was no longer run by debilitating, paralyzing worry anymore.
This did take deeper coaching work together, but it is important to know what is possible when you address the unresolved
stress holding you back in life.)

Sara's case study is a brief glimpse into the ripple effects of her
strength as a mediator and how this survival strategy served
her well in her childhood as well as into her adult life. These
are by no means all of the gifts, but this gives you an idea
of the gratitude and self-appreciation that can begin to arise

when you look at your life from the level of cause and effect and discover the purpose hidden within your pain.

Case Study #2: Laurie

Why Laurie sought support and wanted to work with me:
When Laurie came to see me, she was 49 years old and her life was starting to unravel. She and her husband were close to getting a divorce and she was deeply resentful of how he was not equally pulling his weight in the relationship (neither financially nor in sharing household and parenting responsibilities); meanwhile, Laurie was racing around practically every minute of the day trying to hold everything together. But despite how hard she was working, Laurie never had enough time to be the type of parent she wanted to be while running her business the way she needed to. Laurie knew she had to make changes in her life, but she didn't know how or where to begin. In addition, her once robust health was starting to give out on her. She needed surgery due to a repetitive workout injury, and she had a few other nagging health challenges as well. When Laurie came to see me, she was highly skeptical that I could help, but she was also at her wits end as everything seemed to be on the brink of falling apart.

Laurie's Story:
Laurie grew up in a small city in New Jersey. Up until the age of six, Laurie remembered feeling greatly loved by both of her parents. In particular, she remembered being close with her dad who doused her with love and attention—that was until her parents divorced when she was six and her father moved far away. Laurie did not see her dad for a long time, and when the time finally came to visit him, he had completely changed

towards her. He was no longer the doting father who gave her unconditional love—instead he ignored her for the better part of Laurie's visit while focusing the majority of his attention on his girlfriend. This pattern continued for years. Laurie would visit her father once or twice a year and he would orbit around whichever girlfriend he had at the time while barely acknowledging his daughter. Laurie didn't understand why her dad, who had once made her feel like the center of his world, had suddenly stopped loving her.

With great pain, she wondered what she must have done wrong, and it was at this time, around the age of 7, when Laurie decided (unconsciously) that she was *never* going to let that happen again—she was *never* going to give anyone a reason to abandon her or to stop loving her—and so Laurie became the best at everything she put her mind to. She was a star student, she was great in sports, she was an amazing daughter, and a wonderful friend. She was loved by her mom, teachers, peers, and even her friends' parents greatly admired her hard work ethic, kindness, and generosity. Laurie had a rare gift of being able to make friends quickly among all different social groups. She didn't belong to any click. She saw the good within everyone and had a wonderful ability to make others feel seen and special for who they were. Laurie was very close with her mom and they shared a special bond. But times were hard for her mom as a single parent who struggled to provide financially, so Laurie did her best to not only do well in school, but to help her mom out with cooking, cleaning, and by getting a part-time job. It was incredibly stressful for Laurie to see her mom constantly worrying about finances; she felt her mother's anxiety and took it on as well.

What Were Laurie's Compromised Survival Needs?

Deep down Laurie did not feel that she was unconditionally loved or good enough due to being abandoned, neglected, and ignored by her dad. She also had times of not feeling safe and secure due to her mom's financial stress.

What Survival Strategies did Laurie develop to help get her Survival Needs Met?

perfectionist	workaholic
controlling	critical
networker	responsible
disciplined	ambitious
focused	sought validation from others
comedian	people pleaser
kind	avoided confrontation

Example of Laurie completing Step 3:

Select one of your childhood survival strategies to work with:
Perfectionist (controlling and critical feed into this)

- What need were you trying to get met by being a **perfectionist**?

  Love/Connection   Safety/Security   **Both**

- How did being a **perfectionist** help you to navigate stressful situations in your childhood?

My mom was a single parent and times were stressful for us financially. Being a perfectionist helped me to help my mom - I was self-disciplined, driven and independent. Hard work didn't bother me - I thrived off of it. I wanted to do well to make my mom proud of me and to help take the pressure off her. My mom didn't have to ask me to do chores or to keep up with school - I was mature and on top of my responsibilities. We had an amazing relationship growing up and still do to this day.

- How did being a **perfectionist** help you to improve your ability to get your survival needs of feeling **safe and loved** met while you were growing up?

  My hard work ethic, drive, and discipline were often positively validated with love and praise from my mom, teachers, coaches, and even my friends' parents. I didn't feel loved by my dad, but looking back, I felt loved by my community and certainly by my mom.

  I thrived off doing well and I figured out pretty early on that I could achieve whatever I put my mind to in life.

  Being a perfectionist also helped me to be methodical, strategic, and practical about my future. I hated growing up always stressed out about money. From a young age, I knew I didn't want to live that way and I created a plan of exactly what I needed to do to get into an Ivy League school, and set myself up for a successful future, and that is exactly what I did.

- How has being a **perfectionist** benefited you in your adult life?

Being determined and hard-working helped me to get into one of the best schools in the United States, and when I graduated I was offered a coveted job at an esteemed company. From there my career took off. I spent several years working in the States and later in Europe until I settled back in the US, where I started my own business and became a successful CEO of a multi-national, multi-million dollar company.

- How has being a **perfectionist** helped you in your personal relationships?

    I am an excellent provider and a source of great strength and stability for my family. I am fiercely loving and loyal to my kids. I hold myself to a high standard as a parent and I would move heaven and earth for my children. Because of my success in my career, I am able to give my kids opportunities I didn't get to have while growing up. One of my daughters struggles with health problems and I am able to afford for her to receive excellent therapy and to give her all the resources she needs.

    My closest friends also know that I will be there for them no matter what. I am reliable and thoughtful. I consistently check in with my family and make sure those who are most important to me feel my love and connection.

- How has being a **perfectionist** helped you in your career, health, and finances?

    My perfectionism, drive, and work ethic have put me a cut above the competition and my clients get the results they are paying for. I have a great reputation in my field because I pay acute attention to detail.

My hard work has paid off financially. My business is doing well and I am able to provide a good life for my family. We take several vacations a year, we love to travel outside the country, and I am able to send my kids to great schools. Financially, I came from very little and have created great wealth in my life, which is something I strove to accomplish and is incredibly important to me.

Note:

Laurie's next level of healing was to learn to REFINE and REDIRECT how and when she used her perfectionism, as eventually she was burning herself out and her incredibly high standards were contributing to a breakdown in her health and marriage. But first, Laurie had to own her value. Then from a place of self-appreciation, she was able to learn how to loosen the reigns of her perfectionism and bring greater balance into her life. (You'll learn how to do this in Step 4.)

Bonus: *Laurie's New Healing Perspective*

In our work together, Laurie could see for the first time that the anger and pain she had long felt towards her dad had unknowingly been a powerful catalyst that had brought out the best in her. After reflecting and investigating on the previous five decades of her life, Laurie began to humbly understand that she was where she was in her life and what she was most grateful for—directly because of her fear of being abandoned again.

When Laurie acknowledged WHERE her fear came from, she was able to appreciate that her perfectionism, workaholism, and people pleasing had not only helped her to get where she was in her life, but that they had also been her teachers challenging her to learn an essential life lesson. **Laurie needed to understand on the deepest level of who she was that her TRUE WORTH had nothing to do with her emotionally immature father. He could not be healthy for himself, let alone for her, but most importantly his inability to be a loving father had nothing to do with her inherent value as a human being.** Laurie's self-healing journey was to bring balance to her strengths and to stop overworking herself. She needed to learn to let go enough to let her husband support her more and to stop expecting him to do things exactly how she would do them. She also needed to be okay with delegating tasks that other people could do in her business so that she could focus on her zone of genius, prioritizing actions that only she could take care of in order to increase her company's revenue. In balancing her strengths and stepping into her authentic confidence, Laurie's business took off, she and her husband started getting along better, and they decided not to get a divorce but instead to explore their challenges from a new level of healing and self-accountability. Three years later, Laurie's most recent update is that her income has tripled, her family is still together, and her marriage is stronger than it has ever been.

A powerful way to change your life and open the door for grace to flow in to your day-to-day experience, is to consciously understand that you too can discover the hidden blessings that exist within your pain.

Dr. Viktor Frankl, a world-renowned psychiatrist and author, who survived the Holocaust, put it best when he said:

> *"Suffering ceases to be suffering the moment it finds a meaning. What man needs is not the discharge of tension at any cost, but the call of a greater potential meaning waiting to be fulfilled by him."*

What is the potential meaning waiting to be discovered by you within your adversity?

It's easy to get stuck in the negative perception of how you were wronged or poorly treated growing up, but that only continues **to give your power over to the person who has hurt you the most**. You cannot change what has happened in your past—your power does not lie there—your power lies in you choosing to investigate the empowering ways in which you responded to your adversity. **Step 3 is about taking your power back, owning your value, and no longer allowing your past wounds to continue to hold you back for decades.**

Okay, now that I've shared these two case studies with you, I'd like to invite you to put on your thinking cap. In Step 3, first, you're going to pinpoint which survival strategies you utilized to help you get your survival needs met growing up amidst adversity. Second, you're going to investigate how those survival strategies not only served you well in your childhood, but how they have continued to aid you in valuable ways throughout your adult life.

Step 3: Investigating the Higher Purpose within Your Survival Strategies

Directions:

1. **Important:** For your first time doing this exercise, please only choose ONE survival strategy to work with and then continue on to the next chapter. (If you try to tackle more than one trait this first round, you might get stuck in Step 3 and miss out on how to connect to peace in the Solution Section.)
2. For your first time through, be sure to select a survival strategy that is easier to work with and allows you to discover the hidden benefits more readily. (For example, perhaps choose being a *Problem Solver* over being *Anxious*.)
3. Be gentle with yourself while doing this exercise. Don't put unrealistic expectations on yourself to see all of the higher gifts immediately. This isn't an easy exercise. It takes patience and brain power. So do your best and be kind to yourself. Even if you just see a glimmer of how a survival trait has served you, that will be enough to move on to Step 4.
4. Take 15-30 minutes to do this exercise.

Select one of your childhood survival strategies to work with:

_____

What need were you trying to get met by being

_____?

Love/Connection   Safety/Security   Both

How did being _____ help you to navigate stressful situations in your childhood?

How did being _____ help you to improve your ability to get your survival needs met while you were growing up?

How has being _____ benefited you in your adult life?

How has being _____ helped you in your relationships?

How has being _____helped you in your career, health, finances, and family life?

Before we move on to the next chapter, I want to honor you for showing up to do these exercises and for reading *Anchoring into Grace.*

If you are having a tricky time finding the higher benefits within your survival strategies, know that this is okay and normal. When I ask my clients these tough questions, at first they often draw a blank, but when they stick with the process their intuition and logical mind eventually come together, and they begin to see cause and effect in their lives in profound ways.

So if you are frustrated or being hard on yourself—**I'd invite you to do the opposite**.

I'd invite you to appreciate yourself for even taking the time to read this book and do self-healing work.

You could be doing something else that doesn't require any brainpower—so as simple as it may sound—please give yourself credit for choosing to improve your life! The actions you are taking right now are not small and they can have a positive ripple effect that can elevate every area of your life. So be gentle with yourself as you go through this book.

If you see the value in Step 3 but would like to go deeper in a more fun and supportive way than doing it all on your own, as I mentioned in the last chapter, I have created additional coaching resources, including an online course with videos and a workbook to help take you through each of the traits to uncover your higher gifts, along with video tutorials that explain each chapter in this book. Or, if you'd prefer doing something live, I am offering group coaching programs for people who want to work with me and ask questions in real-time, or you can do transformative coaching work with me in my private 8-week coaching program. Please go to belladodds.com/resources to learn more about these supportive options.

* If you would like to see a short video with several examples of how there are hidden benefits within survival strategies such as: chronic health problems, anxiety, addiction and OCD tendencies, these examples will be available for you for free at: belladodds.com/resources.

To summarize:

In this chapter, you have learned how your survival strategies have aided you well not only in your younger years, but in your adult life as well. In making this conscious, you are valuing and appreciating yourself in ways you may have previously minimized yourself in the past. In so doing, you are authentically building your confidence, which will support you to readily call upon your strengths in healthy ways in the future. In the next chapter, we will focus on how to refine and redirect how and when to use your strengths so that you use your survival strategies in balanced, healthy ways.

Therefore, in working in harmony with your survival program, the next question we want to ask is:

> *How do I work against myself, burn myself out, and try to do the impossible when I use my strengths excessively?*

This next exercise is liberating and can help you to stop the blood, sweat, tear approach, and open the door to work smart, not hard.

Let's dive in.

7

How do I work against myself, burn myself out, and try to do the impossible when I use my strengths excessively?

I love this chapter. It is here where you can begin to learn how to set yourself free and stop trying to do the impossible.

This is how I stopped working against myself and set myself free after five family members passed away, two were diagnosed with cancer, my relationship was unraveling, and a loved one was battling with late stages of alcoholism. During this devastating time, it did not matter how hard I'd tried to make everything okay. The harder I worked, the more unmanageable and painful the situation became.

In order to set yourself free and to start using your strengths in balanced, healthy, and more effective ways, there are two components that are essential for you to understand.

The first component to understand why your strengths start to work against you when you use them excessively is because:

You developed your survival strategies when you were younger, therefore, they are ultimately a child's strategy. This

is why they begin to break down and cause you problems when you default into them too often at the more complex levels of your adult life.

For example, if you had perfectionist tendencies as a child, being a perfectionist was more achievable *because your sphere of responsibilities was smaller and there were not as many things that you needed to be perfect at*. It was manageable to focus your super powers on getting exceptional grades, keeping your room impeccably clean, excelling in extracurricular activities, following the rules, and trying to say and do all the right things. As an adult, however, your perfectionism cannot keep pace with the complexity and pressures of your adult life and the many roles and responsibilities you are juggling each day.

Invariably, you are going to forget to pay a bill. You are going to mess up on an important email. You are going to lose your temper with your kids. You are going to miss a deadline. You are going to say the wrong thing to your partner. You are going to run late. You are going to disappoint someone. You are going to fall short at work. You aren't going to have enough time to get everything done, and there will be days where you will feel that you are in over your head and you may have a li'l meltdown.

Now logically, we all know it is impossible to be perfect — we often say this.

But if we don't consciously up-level this engrained habit of perfectionism to an appropriate, healthy adult strategy — we will unconsciously be compelled to try and be perfect — *even though logically we know it is impossible.*

Interestingly, when you investigate each survival strategy, you can discover that each one is trying to do the impossible. And it is here, in trying to do the impossible, that you uncover a key component that is fueling your overactive survival stress response and causing you to be anxious, tense, irritable, overwhelmed, short-fused, overly hard on yourself, burnt-out, depleted, sad, defeated, exhausted, and frustrated by life's many ups and downs (not to mention possibly contributing to high blood pressure and elevated blood sugar levels).

Fortunately, the solution to self-healing evolutionary dependency is beautiful and life-changing. So take heart as we go through the layers as tremendous good can come out of all of this …

The second component as to why your survival strategies start to work against you and cause you pain and suffering when you use them excessively is because:

They are seeking to control more than is humanly possible in an effort to create a one-sided, pain-free world that does not actually exist.

You will discover when you pull back the layers, underneath the positive intention of each survival strategy, is a powerful desire to avoid unwanted experiences and seek comfort and control. However, the massive problem with this inner need is that *it is in direct conflict with how life actually is*.

No matter how hard you work, you can't finesse life enough to **get your survival needs to feel safe and loved met outside yourself one hundred percent of the time**. Let me give you a clearer idea of exactly what I mean when I say, "we do not live in a one-sided world" so that you will understand the depth to which I am pointing to (rather than it being just a surface-level concept). First, when you look out at the world from an objective point of view, you can clearly see that within the world at large, within nature, and within your personal life—**the physical world is comprised of a multitude of opposites**—and this is true even down to the microscopic domain.

For instance, on any given day, you can personally experience being …

Happy and sad.
Calm and anxious.
Patient and angry.
Healthy and sick.
Confident and doubtful.
You can have people in your life who are reliable, while others can let you down.
You can experience the highs of falling in love, and the lows of breaking up.
You can experience the excitement of getting a new job, and the pain of being fired.
You can experience the joys of being close to your children, and the pain of having them pull away.
(You won't, however, experience a one-sided reality of being happy and stress-free all of the time.)

> *In the coming chapters, we will look at the higher purpose and gifts hidden within duality, but for now, I want to acknowledge the natural world as it is, not as we might wish it to be.*

On a global scale, duality materializes as peace and war.

Progressives and conservatives.
Freedom and slavery.
Corruption and function.
Starvation and gluttony.
Self-interests and integrity.
Cooperation and chaos.
Problem solving and manipulation, and so on.

In the natural world, duality manifests as winter and summer.

Male and female.
Birth and death.
Entropy and syntropy.
Light and dark.
Silence and sound.
Evolution and extinction, and so on.

And perhaps most interestingly, when we explore duality on the microscopic level, we can see that not only does duality exist, *but that it equally plays an essential role in holding the entire physical universe together.*

At the center of an atom, there are positively charged protons that are surrounded by a cloud of negatively charged electrons. These two charges of *attraction and repulsion* create an electromagnetic force that binds an atom together. In turn, atoms build into matter and form infinite manifestations like the Sun, the Earth, the oxygen you breathe, the water you drink, the food you eat, the house you live in, the eyes you see through, and the arms you hug people with.

Humbly, when we observe the laws of physics that give rise to the physical universe, we can see that on the most fundamental level of matter—**without duality all life would cease to exist as we know it**—and the entire physical universe would break apart.

"If electromagnetism was turned off matter would dissolve."
~ Lawrence M. Krauss, Cosmologist

How does understanding the universal law of duality help you to reverse your overactive stress response?

Your survival mode is relentlessly seeking to help you be smart enough, work hard enough, be on top of it enough, make everyone happy enough, get it right all the time enough—so that everything will be okay—24/7.

However, this positive intention, this over-working strategy to make sure everything is okay doesn't actually bear fruit (at least not to the degree that it is intended to).

Take this analogy for example.

Imagine you are standing on the shore of the ocean …

You feel the sand in-between your toes, and as you look out, you see thousands of miles of beautiful water stretched out in front of you as the sunlight glimmers and dances along the surface.

You take a few steps into the ocean and feel the waves come crashing in as you try and keep your balance. As quickly as the waves come in, they recede and you feel a strong undercurrent sucking the water back out into the sea.

For a moment, *imagine you don't like how the undertow throws you off balance.*

And in response to this discomfort and fear—you try and control the ocean and only allow waves to come in—and you do everything in your power to prevent the waves from flowing back out.

Imagine the futility if you actually thought you could do this ...

Now imagine embracing only those circumstances in your life that you like, while simultaneously resisting most of what you don't like. Imagine trying to use your will excessively to force life to be *only as you want it to be.*

How tiring and defeating do you think this constant push-pull with life would be?

Given our health challenges, anxiety levels, conflicts in relationships, battles with depression, and exhaustion, we need to look at the deeper repercussions of how our evolutionary instincts to control and resist the challenging, painful sides of life, are not only futile, but are equally causing us a great deal more suffering than is necessary.

Fortunately, there is a solution ...

What I hope to convey in this chapter is that even though your survival strategies are driven by positive intentions (which aims are to make sure you are safe, secure, and loved) they ultimately cannot work *to the degree that you want them to.* Not because you are failing. Not because you aren't good enough. Not because life is unfair. Not because you aren't working hard enough or because you're falling short—but because no matter how hard you try—your survival program can't defy the laws of nature. You can't work hard enough to nuance your way out of duality. (Even the Dali Lama, one of the world's most renowned spiritual teachers who travels the globe sharing beautiful messages about peace, love, and happiness hasn't been able to return to his beloved home country and sacred Tibetan Buddhist temples for nearly half a century.)

When you look at nature as it is, not as you think it should be, you can see that no matter how much you give and do, you will still experience things that will go your way and things that won't; things you can control and things you can't; you can get it right one minute and make a mistake an hour later. You'll experience both sides of life and so will everyone else.

But what if duality isn't as bad as we think it is and that it's just our unconscious, instinctual response to pain that makes it far worse than it needs to be?

What if embracing duality could actually help us understand how to use our strengths in balanced, healthy ways, and in so doing, free us to create better results in our lives using less effort?

The good news is your body is highly intelligent and can evolve out of survival mode when you consciously teach it a higher, more efficient way to navigate the world.

Step 4 will begin to help you do just that.

> *First*, you will investigate how your strengths work against you when you use them excessively.

> *Second*, you will look at how to use your survival strategies in balanced, healthy, productive ways so that they can enhance your life. (Doing so will also help you to create more time in your day, to be less resentful, to put your own needs first, and to stop exhausting yourself trying to do the impossible.)

To kick this off, I'll give you a quick example of how when I have used my strengths excessively it's led to the opposite effect of my intention ...

Several strengths I have include being tenacious, intuitive, innovative, and good at solving problems. I can intuitively sense the root of an unconscious problem and, through my innovative abilities, find a solution. These skills work exceptionally well when clients hire me to help them figure out what is keeping them stuck or what is wreaking havoc in their lives. My strengths are greatly appreciated in this form and together we go on an inspiring, empowering journey of healing on the deepest level.

However, where my strengths are inappropriate to use is when I sense an underlying problem in a more casual dynamic, say with friends, and I start asking probing questions. Just because I'm intuitive and a good problem solver, doesn't mean it is appropriate to use my abilities in every setting. Not only can this be uncomfortable for people, but it can also be equally draining for me and create dynamics in my relationships that ultimately I do not want. My skills are best used when I am paid to use them or when a friend directly asks for my help.

Additionally, and this was a big one for me, as an environmentalist and humanitarian, I used to feel guilty resting on my laurels for too long. Not only did I care about the world's problems, I also *felt them deeply* and actively wanted to be a part of the *immediate solution* (which meant that I was carrying an underlying, low-level sense of guilt and concern that perpetually gnawed at me). Yet realistically, on a global scale problems are never-ending ... so you can see why it was imperative that I bring my survival strengths of needing to solve problems into balance. Thankfully, I now rest guilt-free, and in fact, I know one of the best things I can do to help the causes I care about is to be strong, take care of myself, and be full on the inside. (I will teach you how to do this in the last section of this book.)

Now, with all of that said, am I perfect at keeping my strengths in balance?

No.

Do I overstep? Yes.

Is it hard not to share something that is right in front of me? Oh hell yeah.

Sometimes I blurt it out (and the people closest to me can hang), but I don't dive into the depths of people's challenges at barbecues like I used to in my twenties, nor am I attached to needing people I love to solve their problems on my timeline. I'm more at peace that we are all on our own journeys through life, and I've learned to honor, recognize, and respect that we each have a time when we are ready to heal. I also humbly know that sometimes a situation needs to get worse before people are ready to do something to improve their situation (if indeed they will ever be ready to change). In truth, none of that is my responsibility, nor is it in my control, and thankfully, now I don't need others to be okay in order for me to feel okay inside myself. (I'll teach you more about this in the Solution Section.)

I'll end my personal experience by saying that when you truly get this … when you truly learn to embrace duality and use your strengths in balance … it is one of the most liberating, healing, and empowering realizations you can come to.

It can release you from debilitating shame, guilt, resentment, and worry.

It can free you from feeling like it is all up to you to make sure that everything is okay.

It can help you to know with clarity why your blood, sweat, and tear approach is not producing the results you want … and you can stop overworking yourself.

It can teach you how to live in harmony with life … and simultaneously open the door for grace to flow into your life in miraculous ways.

It is difficult to convey the relief and freedom that washes over you when you realize you can stop trying to do the impossible … and that in so doing … how your life and others' lives will be the better for it.

So are you ready to dive into Step 4?

I hope so! To help you get the most out of this exercise, I will provide two case studies to help you get your intuitive mojo flowing.

Here are two examples for Step 4:

Select a trait from your survival strategy list: <u>e.g. People pleasing</u>

What is the NEGATIVE effect of using this trait excessively?

- How am I defaulting into being a **people pleaser** too often in my life? How is this working against me and negatively impacting my health, relationships, and joy in life?

The negative effect of trying to make everyone happy - is that it is never-ending. Once I make someone happy, an hour later I have to start all over again. No matter how much I give, it is never enough - I still get criticized. I still end up disappointing someone. In response, I get deeply hurt and even angry when I feel like I have been unappreciated. It sucks that no matter how much I give - I still don't experience the same level of love and care in return. Why don't people think about me with the same thoughtfulness and care that I think about them? I'm sick of experiencing the same script of being hurt, getting resentful, pulling away, and then feeling guilty. It's a never-ending cycle.

I also lose myself when I spend too much time with other people. Sometimes being alone is the only time I can truly rest. Yet this becomes a double-edged sword because it feels like the only time I can breathe easily is when I'm by myself, but when I'm alone for too long I can feel sad, aimless, and lonely.

- How is using **people pleasing** to try and avoid pain or to control people and the outer world ultimately impossible?

  Needing to make sure everyone I care about feels good the majority of the time is ultimately impossible - because I have down days and can be annoyed, hurtful, and selfish too. Why do I think I can prevent people from having the same human emotions and challenges that I have - no matter how much I try to make them happy? Everyone gets stressed out, irritated, grumpy, anxious, hurt, and sad - and there is no way I can prevent the people I love from being in a bad mood with my super-human efforts. There is no way I can do enough to have every person I care about be happy with me all of the time - I've tried for decades and it is not working! I'm tired of wasting my energy trying to do the impossible. I'm tired of being resentful when people don't appreciate me for all that I do. I'm tired of feeling exhausted and putting my needs last. I am tired of taking people's emotions so personally. The majority of the time it's not personal - they are just being human. Maybe their lack of appreciation is life trying to wake me up to stop trying to get my self-worth, approval, and inner peace met through other people.

What is the POSITIVE effect of using this trait in balance?

- How do I want to use being a **people pleaser** in a balanced way? What is a positive, healthy use of this strength?

    The people in my life are incredibly important to me and I want to see them happy. I still want to put care and love in my relationships, but I can see how important it is that I start checking in with myself every day to see how I feel, where I'm at, what my energy levels are, what I want to do, and what my responsibilities to myself are. If I feel tired and depleted, I am going to be mindful not to say yes to things that I don't really want to do or don't have time for. I am going to practice saying no and not feeling guilty about it and try my best to be realistic about how much time I actually have in a day. I am going to remind myself whenever it comes up that I am not responsible for other people being in a good mood. That is their responsibility. I am a good person. I don't have to overextend myself to be loved or to make them happy. I am going to practice giving and receiving equally. I know it feels good for me to give, so I need to let others do the same for me.

With all of this in mind, a healthy use of being a people pleaser is that I enjoy being kind - it feels good. So I will continue to be kind - just not at the expense of being unkind and harmful to myself. I am also a really good listener and care about people and this doesn't have to change. I will use my gifts in balance and continue to invest in having strong, loving, caring relationships, but I will also communicate my needs with others and practice saying no (guilt-free).

- How will my relationships, work, and finances improve when I pull back on **people pleasing?**

My work will improve when I stop overextending myself and taking on other people's workloads. I will put up healthier boundaries and protect my time and energy. I'll close the door to my office and let people know what times I am available and when I'm not. I will try block scheduling so I can focus for an hour or two at a time uninterrupted. In so doing, I will get more done, I will stay more focused, I will do higher quality of work, I will finish sooner, and I will be able to leave at 5:00 and not have to take work home with me. Doing all of the above will give me more energy and time to get my personal responsibilities taken care of, I'll have more time to do things that bring me joy, as well as free up space in my day to spend more quality time with my family.

My finances will also improve as I will have more time to do higher quality work, as well as to stop overspending on others. If I feel better, I can also stop buying things to numb myself out or temporarily make myself feel better.

My relationships will improve when I create healthier boundaries - as I've noticed that when I give too much - the more juvenile and dependent people become on me. In creating healthier boundaries and communicating what I need - I will challenge people in my life to be more mature, and in doing so, I will have healthier relationships with them. It will be better for us both.

- How will my health, energy levels, mental well-being, and my overall experience of life improve when I stop trying to do the impossible?

  I will enjoy my life a lot more! Right now I'm constantly putting out fires, thinking about what everyone else needs, and worrying if they are okay. I can feel a deep emptiness at times ... but I can also sense that I am not far away from feeling a lot better in my life when I start putting myself first more often.

  And when I stop giving 95% of my energy to everyone else and stop trying to do the impossible - I can redirect my freed up energy into areas in my life that NEED MY ATTENTION. I feel something missing inside myself, and instead of staying busy to dull this void, I want to spend more time connecting and tuning in with myself. If I don't acknowledge myself or my needs - why would I expect others to do it if I can't do it for myself? It has to start with me. I look forward to seeing what I'll discover and how I will feel - when I am no longer run by my childhood strategy to please people as a way to get love and create peace.

In the last chapter, we looked at Laurie's perfectionism. Now let's look at how her life improved when she balanced her perfectionism.

Select a trait from your survival strategy list: Perfectionism

What is the NEGATIVE effect of using this trait excessively?

- How am I defaulting into being **a perfectionist** too often in my life? How is it working against me, and negatively impacting my health, relationships, and joy in life?

    At work I can't delegate. I oversee every level of my business and don't trust people to do a good job (or how I want it to be done). The problem with needing to oversee everything or redo things when they aren't done to the level I want is that I am f**king exhausted. I don't have enough time to focus on my family and the areas in my business that only I can do. I also make people walk on eggshells around me. My business could produce two times as much revenue if I would stop trying to oversee every detail and focus on bringing in more clients.

    In my relationships, my husband feels like nothing he does is ever good enough. Over the years he's stopped trying all together and I've just picked up on his slack. This makes me resent him immensely and I am not attracted to him anymore and he's not attracted to me. Our love life has suffered, our connection to each other is greatly compromised, and neither of us is happy. I know it is not all my fault - certainly not - but I can see where making him feel like he is constantly falling short is having the opposite effect of what I want in my marriage.

    As a mom, I don't put my high expectations on my kids like I see some of my friends doing. I let my kids make mistakes and be human, but because I am over-working myself in my business, I don't have enough time to be the type of mom I really want to be. I cannot do it all.

Regarding my health, one of the ways I get my stress out is to go on long runs or workout like a mad woman. At almost 50 my body is not having it anymore - I need to find a new way to have less tension and pressure in my life.

- How is using **perfectionism** to try and avoid pain or to control people and the outer world ultimately impossible?

   I'm not able to enjoy my life. My life is about my to-do list and trying to get everything done. Whenever I fall short, I beat myself up. My need to do everything perfectly is a self-defeating cycle and I have lost my joy and enthusiasm for life. Life and all of my responsibilities feel like a burden - and the only way I can escape is to party pretty hard every so often or to have a few drinks at night to calm down. I've become a bit numb. I am not enjoying my life the way I used to.

   It's also devastating when I get criticized. It feels awful. I need to reflect on how my high standards are making other people feel. I can't be perfect, so how can they?

   My perfectionism makes life feel more like a burden than a meaningful adventure.

What is the POSITIVE effect of using this trait in balance?

- How do I want to use **perfectionism** in a balanced way? What is a positive, healthy use of this strength?

A healthy use of my perfectionism is in my business and specifically with my clients. My attention to detail is great when I am doing important work, but I don't need to oversee every little detail of my business. I have good people on my team. I need to let them spread their wings, do their jobs, and build their confidence. I'll have a meeting with them to get clear on exactly what I need, but how they handle their responsibilities is up to them. We can course-correct as we go and enjoy working together more.

I want to pull back on my perfectionism, criticism, and unrealistic expectations with my husband (it is not working at all). He hates being criticized and so do I. I am going to pick my battles with him on where to offer my opinion or when to make suggestions rather than tell him how to do something. I'd rather have him do more than me do it all by myself (just so I can have it exactly the way I want). I want us to be a team and support each other with more love and kindness like we used to.

- How will my relationships, work, and finances improve if I pull back on **perfectionism**?

*I'll have 20 hours freed up each week by delegating things off my plate that others can do, and instead, I can focus on bringing in new clients. I have a stellar reputation and I am going to keep it this way. Actually, not only will I bring in more revenue, but I'll get better results for my clients because I'll have more time to focus on doing **exceptional** work for them.*

My husband and I can have a reset. I'll let him know what I need his help on and where I am going to pull back on overseeing every detail for our kids and home life. I can talk to him about where my perfectionism and criticism are actually stemming from - from being abandoned by my father (I think he'll appreciate understanding this as he knows how painful that was for me), and that I am consciously going to work on not criticizing him. I won't be perfect at doing it (ha!), but I will actively work on this every day, as it really hurts when he nitpicks me too.

- How will my health, energy levels, mental well-being, and my overall experience of life improve when I stop trying to do the impossible?

  I think I will be able to breathe again. I won't be running around every day frantically trying to do the impossible. I can find more moments of stillness. I can take time for myself and find my joy again. I can focus on healthier ways of relieving my stress and create a new chapter on how I want the next 50 years of my life to be. And I won't beat myself up trying to do the impossible.

Okay, now it is your turn!

Step 4: Use Your Strengths in a Balanced Way

Directions:

1. Go deep with this. Be patient and really give yourself permission to see how you are trying to do the impossible and how your life can change when you use your strengths in balance.
2. Take 15-30 minutes to complete this exercise.

Select a trait from your survival strategy list:

_____

What is the NEGATIVE effect of using this trait excessively?

- How am I defaulting into being _____ too often in my life? How is this working against me and negatively impacting my health, relationships, and joy in life?

- How is using _____ to try and avoid pain or to control people and the outer world ultimately impossible?

What is the POSITIVE effect of using this trait in balance?

- How do I want to use _____ in a balanced way? What is a positive, healthy use of this strength?

- How will my relationships, work, and finances improve if I pull back on _____?

- How will my health, energy levels, mental well-being,

and my overall experience of life improve when I stop trying to do the impossible?

Good work on getting through Step 4!

If this was your first time doing this exercise, please be kind with yourself if you were only able to uncover a few insights. Know that the more you practice pulling back and looking at your life from a level of wisdom and balance, the more insights and epiphanies will reveal themselves to you.

And take the pressure off yourself by remembering that this is a daily practice. It is not a one and done. Don't expect to suddenly use your strengths in balanced, flawless, healthy ways every day, but do have heart knowing that as you practice using your strengths in balance, your life can begin to change with grace.

To summarize:

If you overwork yourself trying to control the outer world (in order to get your survival needs met to feel loved and safe 24/7), you will burn yourself out. It doesn't matter how much you blood, sweat, and tear it, if you resist the universal law of duality, you will pay a heavy price and many of your efforts will begin to work against you. In contrast, when you use your strengths in balanced, healthy ways, you can get far better results in every area of your life while simultaneously using less effort.

Now that you've investigated how duality in the physical world makes it impossible for you to get your survival needs to feel safe and loved met outside yourself 24/7—what is the solution? In the next chapter, we will focus on how it is possible to get your survival needs met on a higher level that offers the consistency and reliability you need.

Therefore, the next question we need to ask is:

> *If my survival needs to feel safe and loved are essential—how can I consistently get my needs met in a world filled with emotional pain, unpredictability, and stressful circumstances that are beyond my control?*

You have reached the Solution Section and the core reason for why I have written *Anchoring into Grace.*

If you take nothing else from this book but what I have to teach you in Chapter 8, I will have done my job.

You're doing great so far. Keep up the good work!

See you in the next chapter.

Section Three:
The Solution

In this section, you will learn how to get your survival needs met on a higher level and connect to an ocean of peace and love that is always available to you, as well as learn how to replenish yourself mentally, emotionally, physically, and spiritually whenever you need to.

8

If my survival needs to feel safe and loved
are essential—how can I consistently get my
needs met in a world filled with emotional pain,
unpredictability, and stressful circumstances
that are beyond my control?

One summer day in the early afternoon, I was surfing the web looking for something light-hearted to watch during my lunch break, when I came across a video that piqued my curiosity between Conan O'Brien and Deepak Chopra.

Conan was interviewing Deepak, and at the start of the interview Conan asked, "You have said you are not afraid of dying. That's a pretty powerful statement. Is there a way all of us can get to that place?"

Deepak responded …

> *"There is a part of you that is not in time.*
>
> *All experience is in time.*
>
> *But the Being that has the experience is not in time.*
>
> *Right now, as you are listening, just turn your attention to who's doing the listening.*
>
> *That presence that you feel.*

That's your Spirit …

It's not in time.

Experience is in time.

Just now, you're having this experience. You'll go somewhere for dinner. You'll have another experience. All experience has a beginning, a middle, and an end.

But the Being … the awareness in which that experience happens … is always a constant."

In hearing Deepak's response, every level of my awareness came to attention. I gently closed my eyes and leaned back in my chair and without thought or effort my consciousness shifted and expanded outward in every direction. As I expanded outward, I felt a deep, vast, rich peace fill and overflow through my body, as my awareness merged with an ocean of life that seemed to stretch out into eternity.

In this infinite, formless, timeless dimension there were no boundaries, no separation between me and everything around me. Only a unified field that was one with everything and everyone. My heart opened and unconditional love poured and overflowed through me.

The level of love that I felt was *more real* and *more alive* than anything in the concrete, physical world.

I felt held by this ocean of pure consciousness …

As I rested in deep peace.

As I rested in weightlessness.

In spaciousness.

In boundlessness.

Being breathed by the universe.

Apart from having one of the most significant spiritual break-throughs in my life come about while watching Conan—how does Deepak's response and my experience tie into how you can get your survival needs to feel safe and loved met in a reliable, practical, and consistent way?

I believe it would be beneficial to explain why I connected into such a beautiful state of peace that day, as it will give you greater clarity on how you can get your survival needs met in a dependable way, amidst the unpredictability of the world. Following this, I'll then take you through a simple exercise to help you to connect to an ocean of peace and love that is available to you at all times.

In short, the reason I believe I went into such a deep level of peace that afternoon is because at the time I was researching evolutionary dependency, and in that moment upon hearing Deepak's response, I experienced what felt like a flash of understanding. In an instant, I could see our collective vulnerabilities as children for the first 15-20 years of our lives; our hyper-vigilant survival strategies; our need for love, safety, and security; our defense mechanisms, and our inability to prevent pain and unwanted experiences from happening. I could see how hard we are on ourselves when we make a mistake and the urgency that grips us when we're trying so hard to make sure that everyone we care about is okay …

And in that moment, a simple opening in my perspective revealed a new possibility and a potential solution.

Yes, I could feel the deeper presence within myself as Deepak had described it.

I had felt this beautiful awareness within me many times before.

This time, however, was different. There was something in the simple way that Deepak explained **the conundrum of time and timelessness existing simultaneously** ... where I suddenly realized ... **that I could consciously experience both simultaneously**.

I could see, feel, and experience the physical world where daily pressures and unpredictability abound; and simultaneously, I could consciously experience myself in the formless spiritual realm where love, serenity, and peace are ever-present. In consciously existing in both of these dimensions at the same time, my body relaxed into a deep state of peace, as it understood that I could get my survival needs to feel loved and safe met *through a means that would always be available to me*. It was so simple, yet my nervous system's response helped me to know that this subtle shift in seeking to get my needs met *inside myself first* — would not only be profoundly significant for my moment-to-moment well-being and long-term physical health — but that it could equally help anyone who wanted to learn how to do this as well.

In that moment, it was clear that each one of us could teach our body's nervous system how to anchor into a source of peace that is available to us at all times (or is 'a constant' as Deepak described it); and in so doing, get our deeper needs met in a consistent and dependable way. Doing so would not only bring more joy, vitality, and beauty into our everyday lives, but it could equally relieve us from being stuck in a state of perpetual stress.

How exactly can the possibility that there is a part of you that does not exist in time—support you in a practical way to feel more calm and peaceful as you go about your daily life?

In the guided meditation we'll be doing shortly (and in the discussion following), we will be exploring the prospect of this notion on a deeper level. This is quite a mystical conversation, but through direct experience and with practice, you can begin to feel and observe for yourself how peace and love are *ever-present states of being.* Equally, you can begin to feel that peace and unconditional love are not dependent on circumstances in the outer world to exist.

Here are a few philosophical questions to activate your higher mind ...

What if peace is available to you at all times, but your senses and survival mode disconnect you from it?

What if you could be fully engaged in the physical realm and simultaneously be anchored in the timeless realm where love, peace, and unity can expand within you?

What if doing so could help your nervous system evolve, thereby supporting you to become better equipped at handling the intensity and demands of the 21st century?

What if you could learn how to rest in eternity for 20 minutes and replenish and reset yourself on a regular basis?

What if you could be connected more often to this ever-present, peaceful, loving, beautiful dimension in a practical, reproducible way?

* * *

As you've learned within this book, your survival program is powerful, and thankfully so, as the job of keeping you alive and safe is certainly an important one. However, most of us aren't navigating true life or death situations in our average day-to-day experiences, which means it is completely unnecessary to have our blood pressure spike fifty plus times a day. To circumvent this, we can do two things. First, we can logically understand that *our survival needs are non-negotiable* (meaning they must be met in order for us to relax and feel calm and okay inside ourselves). And second, we can actively and intentionally seek to meet our needs by tapping into an eternal state of peace and love that is always available to us—and in so doing feel more calm and secure amidst the daily ups and downs of life.

It doesn't mean we'll be perfect at it, nor do we need to be. But we can learn how to embody love inside ourselves even when we are experiencing the opposite in the outer world. If you are more of a visual person, perhaps it would be helpful to look at this concept from this perspective:

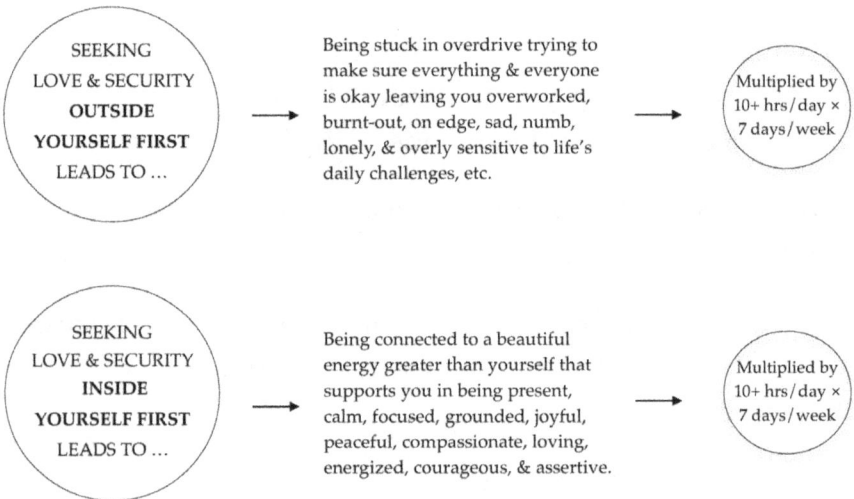

SEEKING LOVE & SECURITY **OUTSIDE** **YOURSELF FIRST** LEADS TO ... → Being stuck in overdrive trying to make sure everything & everyone is okay leaving you overworked, burnt-out, on edge, sad, numb, lonely, & overly sensitive to life's daily challenges, etc. → Multiplied by 10+ hrs/day × 7 days/week

SEEKING LOVE & SECURITY **INSIDE** **YOURSELF FIRST** LEADS TO ... → Being connected to a beautiful energy greater than yourself that supports you in being present, calm, focused, grounded, joyful, peaceful, compassionate, loving, energized, courageous, & assertive. → Multiplied by 10+ hrs/day × 7 days/week

If what I am sharing seems a bit too spiritual, or you are agnostic or an atheist, it might be interesting for you to explore, from a scientific point of view, the evidence that there are indeed dimensions within the universe where time does not exist. A photon of light, for instance, takes approximately 8 minutes and 20 seconds to travel 93 million miles from the surface of the Sun to the Earth. However, *from the photon's perspective, the journey is instantaneous.* A photon of light *does not experience the passage of time* because photons travel at the speed of light and exist in a timeless, spaceless, massless dimension. One notion I think we can all safely agree on is this: *the universe is incredibly mysterious.* So who knows, perhaps within this great mystery, the possibility exists that there is an overlapping correlation between consciousness, light, timelessness, and peace.

For a moment, turn your attention to the deeper presence within you. Close your eyes and notice …

Does the deeper presence within you feel dull or awake?

Does your witnessing awareness feel solid or does it have a buoyant, formless quality to it?

Does the deeper presence within you live in the past or in the future — or does it feel fully alive, awake, and aware in the present moment?

Does the deeper presence within you feel timeless?

Can you pinpoint where your consciousness ends and where it begins?

Up until now, everything in this book has been intellectual, more of a mental exercise, but now it is time for you to experience how to physically and emotionally connect to peace and love with greater ease in your everyday life.

To teach you how to connect to an ocean of calming energy that is a constant and is always available to you, I will guide you through a simple exercise. I take each of my clients through this process in our first session together, and to offer the same level of one-to-one support, I have recorded a guided meditation for you. The benefits of being guided through this process with your eyes closed, rather than having to read through it, will help you to connect to a peaceful, higher state of awareness with far greater ease and effectiveness.

**To listen to this free guided meditation
please go to belladodds.com/peace**

If you think you'd rather read through the exercise, I have transcribed it for you below. With that said, my advice is not to do both, at least not at first. If you sense you would like to listen to the exercise, it is best to listen to it before reading through the transcript, so as not to have your logical mind interfere with the simplicity and grace of the experience.

Additionally, while you are doing the exercise, please take the pressure off yourself and **let go of any expectations of what you think you 'should' experience**. You don't need to merge with profound levels of peace to be doing this right. If all you feel is a bit more calm and relaxed during the exercise then that is a wonderful starting point. Know that even a small ray of peace is enough to ease the burden of stress within you, and the gentle presence of love can give you the buoyancy you might need if you are feeling depleted and disconnected. Just be patient and kind to yourself as you learn something new, and allow yourself to be open to the possibility that these beautiful states of consciousness exist at every moment and are inseparable from who you really are. And the good news is that the more you practice, the more natural it will become for you to connect to the ever-present ocean of peace and love within you.

> "Your task is not to seek for love,
> but merely to seek and find all the barriers within
> yourself that you have built against it."
>
> ~ Rumi

Step 5: Connecting to Peace and Unconditional Love

Directions:

1. This exercise will take about 15 minutes.
2. I am going to guide you through two doorways that will assist you in connecting to peace and unconditional love. Try both and see which doorway creates a stronger connection for you and which is more natural for you to use.
3. Know it will become easier to connect to these higher states of consciousness the more you practice and the more your nervous system learns it is safe and beneficial to let go and do so.
4. This exercise is simple.
5. Let it be simple.

Part 1: Listen to the guided meditation at belladodds.com/peace

Close your eyes and take a nice deep breath in …

And exhale.

Now say to yourself I am calm.

My mind is calm.

My body is calm.

Inhale again …

Exhale slowly …

Gently allow tension in your body to begin to melt away.

Breathe in again and exhale.

Now I'd like you to gently think of a peaceful place in nature. It can be a place you've been to that you love, or it can be a place that comes to your mind that you think of as calming.

Trust whatever place comes to you.

Be there now.

Be in this peaceful place and breathe in.

Allow yourself to take in and enjoy this relaxing, healing place.

Let yourself breathe in the beautiful, rich, peaceful energy of nature for a few breaths.

Notice how you feel inside yourself.

Do you feel lighter or heavier?

Do you feel more spacious and expansive?

Is your mind racing or is it relaxed?

Can you sense a presence of peace within you?

In this moment, do you feel safe?

In your mind's eye, see the beauty of this peaceful place again.

Be there now.

Feel its calming, serene energy.

Breathe in this peaceful energy and let yourself rest in this healing place.

Allow peace to fill and overflow through you.

Now notice … does this peaceful energy feel dense or does it have a formless quality to it?

Within this lighter, peaceful energy, can you sense a presence of love within it?

If you can, beautiful. If you can't right now, beautiful.

Whatever you feel is right and good for you. We'll do another exercise to feel love shortly. Just notice what you notice. You're doing great.

Again be in this beautiful, peaceful place in nature.

Breathe in its serenity and allow yourself to be relaxed, light, and spacious.

In feeling the peace within yourself, can you sense how this energy is one with you … that peace is not separate from you, but that this peace is within you and a part of you?

This beautiful, light, expansive energy that you feel … this is your Soul's energy.

Your Soul is one with peace.

Notice the expansive, boundless presence and awareness of your Soul.

Notice how alive and aware you feel.

Feel the beauty of who you really are that has nothing to do with the outer world.

Notice … is your mind in the past or future, or is it in the present?

Your Soul lives in the eternal present.

Feel the value of peace within you. You didn't have to do anything in the world to be valuable—you are already infinitely valuable.

You didn't have to do anything in the outer world to create safety.

Your Soul is calm, loving, and powerful and it is not afraid.

Okay, beautiful. While keeping your eyes closed, take a deep breath in and gently move your arms, body, and head from side to side.

Good job, you're doing great.

We're going to explore another doorway into healing energy.

Now I would like you to think about an animal or person in your life that you love deeply.

This animal or person can be alive or have passed …

Please only choose an animal or person that makes you feel good when you think about him or her. This exercise will not be effective and can be counterproductive if you select an animal or person that you have emotional grief, sadness, worry, resentment, or anxiety around. Instead, you want to choose an animal or person that you have a beautiful relationship with and feel unconditional love, lightness, and happiness when you think about this Soul.

Many people have had a beautiful relationship with an animal in their lives and find pets easier to work with in this exercise, but if you don't have a good connection with a pet, you can choose a family member, friend, teacher, or someone in the world who inspires you or who you deeply love.

Now take a deep breath in and think of this animal or person.

Feel your gratitude for them

Feel your love for them.

Imagine giving this animal or person a hug and giving all your love to them.

Feel this Soul being grateful for your love and loving you right back.

Can you feel the presence of love within you … even if it is just a subtle feeling?

If the presence of love is subtle … let it build.

Let your love for this animal or person fill and overflow through you.

Let this love expand and deepen inside you.

Notice in this moment ... do you feel empty or full?

Does this loving energy have a formless and spacious quality, or does it feel solid?

Does this loving energy expand a bit beyond your body?

Does this loving, formless energy feel interconnected to the world around you in any way ... if so, how far out does love go?

Does love feel like it is in the past or future, or does it feel like it exists in the eternal present?

Just notice what you notice.

Take a deep breath in.

Exhale.

Focus again on your love and gratitude for the animal or person in your life.

Fill your whole being with unconditional love for them.

Notice in feeling your love for this Soul ... is love separate from you?

Or is love *one* with you?

Can you feel that love is connected to you on the deepest level ... that love is inseparable from who you are?

Allow yourself to breathe in the lightness of love. Let this love fill and expand inside you.

Focus again on the animal or person you love.

Feel your tremendous gratitude for them.

Give them a hug and show your appreciation.

Allow your love to grow and expand inside you.

This loving, expansive presence is your Soul's energy.

You are not separate from love.

You are made of love.

There is nothing you need to do to be worthy of love … love is the ever-present light of who you really are.

There is nothing you need to do to be more valuable.

You are already immeasurably valuable.

In being connected to this loving presence … can you sense that this beautiful energy loves you too?

Can you sense that you don't need someone else to validate your worth, because you are already unconditionally loved and seen by the Source of life that created you?

Your Soul's value has nothing to do with the outer world.

No one can take away or diminish your light or true worth.

You are and have always been valuable.

You are and have always been unconditionally loved.

Let yourself rest in the spaciousness of love for a few breaths.

Beautiful job.

Okay, gently move your arms, hands, legs, and head from side to side.

Take a deep breath in.

Exhale and gently open your eyes.

Part 2:

1. Please write down your experience in connecting to these higher states of consciousness. How did you feel? What did you perceive? What did you notice?
2. If you resonate with the sentiment that you have a Soul, what did you perceive in being connected with this expansive, eternal part of yourself?
3. In the meditation, did you find connecting to peace or connecting to love to be more natural for you?

> For instance, some of my clients find that they can connect and deepen into peace more easily (or they feel more calm and relaxed when they connect to nature), but they struggle a bit connecting to the presence of love. If you experienced this as well, don't worry. This is not uncommon at first. In some cases, my clients have shared that because they did not feel unconditionally loved growing up, they have questioned trusting their ability to know what love feels like. If you experienced something similar, **know that connecting to peace can be a graceful doorway into experiencing the greater depths of love over time**.
>
> If this is the case for you, I would suggest taking the pressure off yourself for now, and instead of trying to connect to love, practice connecting to peace first. In time, you will trust knowing what love feels like and

you can begin to feel the lightness of love expanding within you naturally. This is where grace will come in. You don't have to figure it all out on your own or try to force this. Simply keep practicing and allow the room for the wisdom of life to work with you.

I hope you found this exercise to be helpful and enjoyable. If you struggled with it or found using the two focus points of a loved one or nature to be tricky, I have created a third exercise you can try using the visualization of light. (This guided meditation is also available for you at belladodds.com/peace)

One reason I chose to take you through this specific exercise is because many of us have not been taught how to connect to higher states of consciousness simply *by using our focus and intention*. The good news is that *each one of us knows how to connect … as peace and love are inseparable from who we are on the deepest level*. With that said, we do need to practice simple techniques like this in order to pull our senses back from the world and strengthen our 'inner connection muscle.' Fortunately, connecting to peace and love doesn't have to be complicated — animals and nature are wonderful teachers that can help us learn how to connect with greater ease — as well as take our self-doubt out of the equation and simplify the learning process for us. In time and with practice you won't even need to close your eyes or be by yourself in order to connect. You will be able to embody these higher states of consciousness anytime, anywhere simply by shifting your inner awareness and focus.

———————

Embodying the expansive presence of peace and love and reading about them are two different things.

In this section, I will do my best to describe how the higher states of consciousness of love and peace can greatly support you. But know that whatever words I use to describe these healing energies, there are no intellectual concepts that can fully do justice to the beauty, depth, and impact they can have in your life. For this reason, I will point to what embodying peace and love can do for you.

First, how are love and peace available to you at every moment?

In the guided meditation, you did not have to physically go to a peaceful place in nature in order to be able to tune into peace and feel it expand within you. (Nor did you have to get everything done on your to-do list, or make someone be happy with you in order to relax and feel okay.)

Likewise, you did not have to change circumstances in your life in order to feel peaceful in that moment; you simply connected inward and used the *power of your focus* to tune into peace, which is an ever-present state of being that is inseparable from who you really are. In so doing, you helped your body feel safe and you got your survival needs met through a higher level of awareness (which is possible for you to do even when you are under a great deal of stress).

How does embodying peace help you to get your survival need to feel safe met?

I can attempt to give you an intellectual answer, but it would be more powerful for you to feel this truth within yourself.

The next time you do this exercise or when you feel peaceful and calm, check in with yourself and gently ask:

In feeling peace inside myself ... do I also feel at ease?

In feeling at ease ... do I also feel safe and okay in this moment?

The chances are good that if you feel peaceful or relaxed, you will also feel safe *in that moment* (otherwise you'd probably be tense, irritable, anxious, or on edge to some degree). Consequently, one solution to stop living with relentless stress **is to learn how to feel safe and secure inside yourself first.**

When you practice embodying peace within (regardless of what's going on around you), you can ...

- Calm your mind and body down.
- Let go of holding on so tightly and soften your thinking.
- See situations more clearly and wisely.
- Feel safe and secure on a deep level.
- Experience your mindfulness, prayer, and meditation practice to be more effective.
- Breathe more easily and deeply (helping to lower your blood pressure).
- Feel more centered and anchored in your body.
- Be more present and less reactive.
- Take situations less personally.
- Move through your day from a grounded, wise presence (instead of frantically going about your day run by urgency, tension, or worry).
- Live with an open heart.
- Be connected to your Soul.
- Feel supported by an energy greater than yourself.

- Open the door for grace and synchronicities to flow into your life.
- Connect to and hear your intuition more strongly.
- Trust in the higher good that is unfolding in your life.
- Embody a deeper knowing that all will be okay, even if in that moment the outside world seems to be upside down.
- Pull back on over-using your survival strategies and trying to control more than is humanly possible.
- Be less sensitive to the moods and emotions of people around you.
- Feel the underlying beauty and luminous energy within all things.

You can't control the outer world, but you can practice embodying security and peace within yourself. When you do so, your brain waves can slow down, your breathing can deepen, your blood pressure can go down, and you can stop thinking of fifty things that you urgently need to get done all at once. Instead, you can calmly plan your day and take steady action. Not from a place of overwhelm, but from a place of equanimity ... or as Lao Tzu once beautifully shared,

"Nature does not hurry, yet everything is accomplished."

How does embodying love help you to get your survival need to feel loved met?

During the guided meditation, you did not have to change anything in the world around you, be physically held by someone, or be in the presence of a loved one in order to feel love expand inside you. (Nor did you have to accomplish something great or be praised in order to feel valued and seen.) You simply used the *power of your focus* to tune into the state of consciousness of love that is ever-present and is inseparable from who you really are.

As you strengthen your ability to connect to and embody love, you are simultaneously getting your survival need met to be loved, which supports your survival mode to feel secure and at ease. (It is possible to feel unconditionally loved even when you are being rejected or criticized, or when you've messed up, or you have temporarily failed. Instead of spiraling down in negativity, you can pause, reset yourself, and connect to a healing presence that loves you unconditionally. Your parents or your partner might not be able to love you uncondition-ally—but the mysterious Source of consciousness giving you life—*does love you unconditionally*. The more you practice con-necting to the presence of love—the more you can feel and know this to be true on a deep level.)

When you practice embodying unconditional love within you (regardless of what is going on around you), you can ...

- Feel the immeasurable value and light of who you really are expanding within you.
- Live with an open heart.
- Move with a lightness of being.
- Be more joyful.
- Be more kind and compassionate.
- Feel more calm.
- Strengthen your intuition.
- Stand up for those who need support.
- Radiate vitality.
- Take decisive action, live courageously, and follow your inner-compass.

- See the light and inherent value within you and within others.
- Know your true worth has nothing to do with the outer world or what people think about you.
- Feel and know that you are unconditionally loved (for the whole of who you are—including your struggles and weaknesses).
- Stop overworking or overextending yourself trying to get your value met outside yourself first.
- Stop compromising your boundaries, exhausting yourself, or being dependent on others for validation, praise, or for your sense of identity.
- Feel the beauty of love within you and within all things.
- Be connected to your Soul.
- Feel how you are connected to everyone and everything … including the rivers, trees, animals, blades of grace, vast oceans, and distant stars.
- Experience unity consciousness.

As you practice connecting to love and feeling the deeper presence of who you really are, you can know that your true worth has nothing to do with the outer world or what others think of you. From here you won't need to overwork or over-give in order to seek outer validation. Instead, you can tap into the infinite source of love and allow it to fill and overflow through you, thereby embodying your innate worth (which you may have forgotten). Through feeling the light and beauty of who you really are … your sensitivity to criticism can abate … as you know your true worth cannot be diminished by the judgments of others.

"Remember, the entrance door to the sanctuary is inside you."

~ Rumi

Why don't I experience peace and love more easily in my day-to-day life if these states of consciousness are one with who I really am?

One reason it can be difficult to connect to the peace within you is because your body's central nervous system evolved in the physical world and it is designed to be hyper-vigilant and is constantly scanning your environment to keep you alive. (Think of a gazelle in the field.) In addition to this, during the first 15-20 years of your life you were vulnerable and highly dependent on others to get your survival needs met. For both of these reasons, your nervous system learned to navigate the world by being overly sensitive, focused, and tuned in to what was going on around you. In so doing—this simultaneously resulted in you disconnecting and weakening your felt-connection to the presence of grace within you—as your body's dominant objective was on outer world survival first.

In hopes of making clear the true impact the healing energies love and peace can have in helping you to get your survival needs met in a reliable way, let's look at the question I posed at the beginning of this chapter one more time:

If my survival needs to feel safe and loved are essential—
how can I *consistently* get my needs met in a world filled
with emotional pain, unpredictability, and stressful
circumstances that are beyond my control?

Living in a world of duality means that we cannot get our survival needs met solely and primarily outside of ourselves *one hundred percent of the time.* Therefore, if we no longer wish to live with relentless stress, if we no longer wish to have the outer world dictate how we feel on the inside, if we no longer want to waste our energy trying to control more than is humanely possible, if we want to stop seeking validation from others, if we want to stop defaulting into survival mode and feeling overly anxious, irritable, resentful, and exhausted **we must learn how to embody feeling safe and loved inside ourselves FIRST.**

We must learn to consciously evolve and get our needs met on a higher level.

Now, just because it may not be easy to connect to the higher states of peace and love anytime and anywhere … *doesn't mean you don't innately know how to do it.*

Rather, it points to two things:

> *One,* you most likely need to strengthen your 'inner-connection' muscle after being predominantly outer world focused and anchored for decades.

> *Two,* you can begin to strengthen your ability to connect to love and peace through daily practice.

The good news is that your nervous system is ready to evolve when you are.

You are the captain of your ship.

You can consciously teach your body, mind, and emotions how to get your survival needs met inside yourself first. In the beginning, you will mostly likely need to practice strengthening your ability to connect to peace and love by using the guided meditation to direct your focus on nature, animals, or a loved one (or with a variety of other mindfulness and breathing techniques that are widely available); but with time and practice, it will become easier to connect to these healing energies simply by using your intent and focus … anytime, anywhere.

The next chapter will be dedicated to doing just that. You'll learn a few simple techniques on how you can practice anchoring into grace as you go about your busy day.

Why do I sometimes feel anxious or experience an increase in uncomfortable emotions when I'm trying to meditate, pray, or be mindful?

One reason you might feel more anxious or uncomfortable when you are meditating or being mindful is because *your body and mind can actually be in conflict with each other*. For instance, if you consciously want to relax, let go, and feel at ease—but your body doesn't feel safe deep down—can you see how trying to relax would create an inner-conflict between your conscious desire and your subconscious mind? Your conscious desire may be to relax, but your body's survival program is wanting to keep you safe and secure. Consequently, your body will be geared toward alert mode. As a result of this, instead of feeling more calm as you meditate, you may experience the opposite. You might be filled with a heightened sense of anxiety or other unpleasant emotions that can be extremely uncomfortable and overwhelming.

Thankfully, you can *work in harmony with this inner-turbulence* by understanding that your anxiety might actually be a message from your body that deep down you don't feel safe or secure about something in that moment—or your sadness might be a message from your body that you feel disconnected, lonely, or you don't feel good enough about something in your life. If this is the case, your survival program will be focused on finding a solution (typically through resourcing one of your lead survival strategies).

The good news is that when you understand the *positive intention* of your survival program—the practice of meditating, praying, or being mindful becomes a beautiful solution! The difference is that you are now conscious of the complexity going on inside you—and instead of being overtaken by your emotions—**you can hear and decipher what you need deep, deep down**. And it is through this conscious understanding that you can use your meditation, prayer, or mindfulness practice to bring your pain to the light; to allow your fears to be held by the healing presence of peace; to merge your loneliness with the soothing presence of unconditional love; to surrender your pain to a healing energy that is greater than yourself, and in so doing, open the door for grace to flow into your life.

In essence, what I am suggesting is a *subtle shift in your intention*. One where you don't see your anxiety, stress, or intense emotions as being overwhelming or a sign that you are doing something wrong. But rather, it is where you compassionately understand and honor your basic survival needs, *and actively work in harmony with your body to practice getting your needs met on a higher level.*

If you are not a spiritual person, or if you have more of a scientific mind, let's look at connecting to peace, love, and joy as it relates to your health from a biological perspective.

Scientific studies referenced in Dr. David Hamilton's book, *How Your Mind Can Heal Your Body,* reveal that humans live longer and are physically healthier when they experience more uplifting emotional states:

> *"In 2003, scientists at Duke University Medical Center, on examining 866 heart patients, discovered that the patients who routinely felt more positive emotions (e.g. happiness, joy, and optimism) had about a 20% greater chance of being alive 11 years later than those who experienced more negative emotions. And in a 2007 study, Harvard scientists studied the effects of 'emotional vitality,' which was defined as 'a sense of positive energy,' an ability to regulate emotions and behavior, and a feeling of 'engagement in life.' The study involved 6,265 volunteers and found that those who had high levels of emotional vitality were 19% less likely to develop coronary heart disease than those with lower levels." (5)*

Other studies reveal that meditation can have a positive impact on our physiology as well, which is one reason I became certified to teach *Primordial Sound Meditation* through the *Chopra Center*. Remarkably, this simple form of self-transcending meditation has been shown through various scientific studies that merging with higher states of consciousness can help:

- Decrease activity in the amygdala (responsible for our body's fight, flight, freeze response).
- Promote greater brain coherence and function.
- Support our body's immune system.
- Lower our blood pressure and help balance our blood sugar levels.
- Improve our quality of sleep.
- Decrease inflammation and systemic pain throughout the body.

- Increase the length and health of our telomeres (connected to cellular renewal and longevity).
- Decrease anxiety and depression.
- Increase inner peace and joy.

Our bodies don't lie.

On a biological level they reflect back to us that feeling more positive emotions in our lives, not only benefits our mental and emotional well-being, but these higher emotional states are equally necessary for our long-term physical health.

Our survival program was not designed to be chronically switched on. It was designed for life or death situations, and it is incredibly hard on our health when we live in a perpetual state of tension and stress. Research has shown that the overactive stress response can increase our risk of diabetes, heart disease, strokes, and cluster symptoms.

> (Cluster symptoms include having five or more symptoms from a list of over forty seemingly unrelated health challenges such as: stubborn weight, infertility, hormonal imbalances, eczema, psoriasis, arthritis, headaches, allergies, difficulty sleeping, anxiety, depression, digestive problems, difficulty concentrating, fatigue, auto-immune diseases, thyroid imbalances, etc. If you would like to learn how a myriad of health problems can be linked to the overactive stress response, as well as to four other root causes, I recommend reading, *The Adrenal Thyroid Revolution* by Dr. Aviva Romm.)

Without question, based on the shocking rise of physical, mental, and emotional health problems, it has become crystal clear that we need to learn new ways to help our nervous system, mind, and emotions feel more safe and secure in the over-stimulating, fast-paced 21st century world. Whether you relate to peace and love as spiritual energies, or if you see them as hormones created by your brain, what is essential to understand is that these higher states of consciousness are vital for your health, longevity, and well-being on all levels.

Thankfully, you can teach your body how to evolve out of survival mode and to embody peace even amid uncertainty—you can tap into the ever-present state of love even when you are being rejected—and you can trust that everything will be okay in the long-run even when you're enduring great challenges.

Having healed debilitating anxiety myself, I can say that I am no longer run by compulsively needing to prevent, solve, or do something in the outer world in order to feel a level of safety within me; nor must I achieve, be validated, or loved by someone in order to feel love and know that I am loved. I am no longer run by my childhood dependency of constantly needing to improve or influence my environment to determine how I feel on the inside. Instead, I resource these healing energies directly from within, as love and peace are a constant and they are one with the deepest level of my being.

Am I perfect at it?

No.

And I don't need to be.

But I do need to connect each day and be full and strong on the inside in order to better surf the ups and downs of my daily life (I will teach you how to monitor how full and strong you are in chapter 10).

The good news is that there is nothing in this chapter that I am sharing with you that you can't already do or learn how to do. Being able to embody peace on a deep level is not a unique ability reserved for the few. Life will go upside down and sideways, but you too can practice being strong on the inside no matter what is happening around you. You too can replenish yourself mentally, emotionally, physically, and spiritually throughout the day. And as you strengthen your ability to feel love and peace expand within you … you may find that these healing energies become your teachers … awakening you, guiding you, and restoring you on the deepest level of who you really are.

Do you have to be connected to peace at all times to be 'doing this right'?

I don't believe it is necessary, healthy, or realistic to be peaceful all the time. We are here to experience the full range of human emotions, not to spiritually bypass our shadow and pretend that all is well when it isn't. Heavier emotions are our teachers too. They give us vital feedback on what we need to become aware of and what needs healing within ourselves (we'll explore this important and meaningful topic in greater detail in the last chapter).

As I've said, I don't live in a constant state of peace and unconditional love. Anyone who knows me knows that I get emotional, over-react, defend, and protect myself. I am learning and growing just like everyone else; however, I don't stay off-center or self-righteous for too long. I don't spin out for days and weeks. I learn how to stop, connect, and replenish myself with healing energy. Once I've taken time to quiet my mind and be connected to the ocean of stillness within me, I am able to humble myself, surrender, and embrace the lesson being given to me … while feeling equally supported by a wise loving presence that is far greater than myself.

So keep in mind that there is no pressure here to be perma-peaceful or a Buddhist Monk!

Instead you are exploring how it is possible to feel more secure, serene, and loved inside yourself more often … regardless of what is going on around you … so that you can get off the hamster wheel and enjoy your life with greater richness, joy, vitality, and meaning. Jon Kabat-Zinn shared this notion beautifully in his book, *Falling Awake*,

> *"The invitation is always the same: to stop for a moment— just one moment—and drop into wakefulness. That is all. Stop and drop: meaning, drop into your experience of experiencing, and for even the briefest of moments, simply holding it in awareness as it is—in no time, or to put it differently, in this timeless moment we call now, the only moment we actually ever have … None of this means that you won't get things done. In fact, when your doing comes out of being, when it is truly a non-doing, it is a far better doing and far more creative and even effortless than when we are striving to get things done without an ongoing awareness moment by moment. When our doing comes out of being, it becomes an integral and intimate part of a love affair with awareness itself."*

In the next chapter, we'll be practicing how to *stop and drop* into the present moment amidst your daily busy life. To help make this practical, I'll teach you another simple, mindbody exercise on how to anchor into grace using a light bathing technique. This simple technique can help strengthen your ability to feel serene as you're driving to work, shopping at the grocery store, or when you're around someone who's in a bad mood.

In summary

In order to feel more calm, energized, and confident as you go through your life, you can teach your body, mind, and emotions how to connect to the healing energies of peace and love that are ever-present and always available to you (regardless of what is going on around you). In so doing, you will be able to get your survival needs met to feel safe and loved through a more reliable, consistent source. Which means that even if it's a hard day, even if someone is disappointed in you, even if a loved one is in a bad mood, or you've made an error at work—you can learn how to resource feeling calm and okay inside yourself. Over time, this can support you to being strong and full within—and replace burnout, frustration, and overwhelm—with greater levels of joy, vitality, and confidence.

We explored quite a bit in this chapter! Now we want to simplify it and make it real in your everyday life. And that leads us to the next question:

How can I embody peace and love when I'm on the go and overly busy trying to get everything done?

Time for some good ol' fashioned light bathing and serenity ...

See you in the next chapter!

9

How can I embody peace and love when I'm on the go and busy getting things done?

What you focus on and think about greatly informs how you experience your moment-to-moment reality. You can focus on everything that isn't going your way and mentally stew for hours getting more and more upset about what a person did to you or what someone said to you. You can be gripped in angst worrying about the uncertainty of the future, or you can be filled with guilt if you said or did the wrong thing, etc. On the flip side, you have the option to not let your mind run unabated and instead reclaim the power of your focus. The steps within the *Anchoring into Grace Method* will help you to reclaim your mind because as you become more aware of what survival needs you are trying to get met at any given moment—you can consciously begin to recognize that it *those unmet needs* that are greatly contributing to your stress.

For example, if you notice yourself tensing up, you can check in and ask:

What am I grappling with right now?

What am I really upset or worried about?

Underneath this stressful circumstance—deep down—do I feel strain around not feeling safe and secure, or am I upset that I don't feel loved, respected, seen, or accepted for who I am?

In realizing that something in the outer world is compromising one of your survival needs, you can pause, breathe, and connect to the presence of unconditional love and peace within you. When you do this, you interrupt the endless stream of stressful thoughts and emotions gripping you. And instead, you give yourself a chance to slow down and get your survival needs met on a higher level, and in doing so, empower yourself to feel more calm and secure inside yourself (even though nothing has changed in the world around you). After a few seconds or a few minutes of connecting to peace, you can re-engage with your current discomfort from a more calm, wise, and secure perspective.

In this chapter, we'll be exploring a few simple techniques of how to center yourself and connect to deeper levels of peace, security, and love within you as you go about your normal day-to-day life. To support you in this process, I've created a simple mindbody exercise on *Light Bathing* to help strengthen your nervous system's ability to connect to peace.

Step 6: Anchoring into Grace

Directions:

1. This exercise will take about 10 minutes.

2. **For more effective results please go to belladodds.com/peace to be guided through this calming meditation with music.**

Part 1: Light Bathing

Get into a nice comfortable position.

Take a deep breath in and close your eyes …

And exhale.

Now say to yourself I am calm.

I am calm.

Inhale calm

Exhale calm.

I am calm.

I am calm.

Inhale calm.

Exhale calm.

My mind is calm.

My body is calm.

I am peaceful.

I am peaceful.

My mind is peaceful.

My body is peaceful.

Inhale peace.

Exhale peace.

In your mind's eye see a pool of beautiful, calming, healing water in front of you.

The water is warm, soothing, and the perfect temperature.

You take a step in with one foot and then the other.

The healing water gently relaxes your bones, muscles, and nerves as your feet tingle and then relax.

You take a few more steps into the healing pool as the water rises up to your hips and gently relaxes your bones, muscles, and nerves as your legs tingle and become deeply relaxed.

You take a few more steps in up to your chest as the healing water gently relaxes your bones, muscles, organs, spine, ribs, heart, and nerves as your upper body and arms tingle and become deeply relaxed.

Now effortlessly, you naturally begin to float, as your head, neck, and body are supported by this calming, healing water.

As you float, you become more and more relaxed.

Now you see a golden cup above you … and this golden cup is filled with liquid, healing light.

This golden cup gently pours healing light into your body as you feel the light flowing into your hips and legs and out through your feet.

The golden cup begins to gently pour liquid healing light into your abdomen and heart as the light fills and overflows through you.

Wherever you feel emptiness, darkness, fatigue, pain, or stress in your body … this healing, liquid light brings light to the darkness and fills and overflows through you.

The liquid, healing light pours and flows up through your neck and head filling your whole being with a healing, luminous light.

As you breathe in, you feel lighter and lighter.

Now say to yourself … I am calm.

I am calm.

I am filled with light.

My mind is filled with light.

My body is filled with light.

My heart is filled with light.

Breathe in light.

Exhale light.

I am filled with light.

Allow each of your cells to bathe in light.

Allow each of your cells and every fiber of your being to be nourished and revived in this luminous, healing light.

Breathe in light.

Exhale light.

Let it feel good.

Let it feel beautiful.

Let it feel healing.

Now say to yourself …

I am peaceful.

My mind is peaceful.

My body is peaceful.

Gently float in this healing light for a few breaths …

Now you feel the light gently begin to lift you up out of the water and onto a soft, comfy reclined chair.

You are warm, dry, comfortable, and relaxed.

Notice the lightness and spaciousness within you.

Feel the formless, expansive, peaceful consciousness within you.

Take a nice deep breath in …

And exhale.

Now before opening your eyes, ask yourself …

How do I want to re-enter the world?

Take another nice deep breath in …

Exhale.

Do I want to feel peaceful and calm?

Do I want to be kind?

How do I want to move through my day?

Take another nice calming breath in.

And exhale.

Now gently and slowly move your head from side to side.

Gently and slowly move your legs from side to side.

Softly and gently open your eyes.

See if you can stay connected to the beautiful, spacious, peaceful energy within you as you re-enter the world.

Today practice re-connecting to the peace within you and coming from kindness.

Practice taking moments out of being on automatic pilot and come from your Soul's essence of love, lightness, and serenity as you move through the world.

Beautiful job.

Part 2: Practice Anchoring into Grace 5-20 Minutes Every Day

Living from the inside out means that you are learning how to resource your survival needs to feel safe and loved inside yourself first. To strengthen your ability to connect to peace, you can make it simple by practicing one of the exercises of focusing on nature, an animal, a loved one, or light bathing (or any other mindfulness, prayer, breathing, or meditation technique that you might enjoy).

With practice, these exercises will help you to strengthen your inner-connection muscle and fine-tune your ability to connect to love and peace when you're on the go. The good news is, the more you practice connecting, the easier it will become to embody these higher states of consciousness anytime, anywhere.

To strengthen your inner-connection muscle, practice connecting to and filling your body with love, peace, and light for 5-20 minutes every day for at least two weeks.

To do so:

- Get into a comfortable position and take a few deep breaths in and out to center yourself.
- Next, listen to one of the guided meditations on: light bathing, connecting to nature, an animal, or a loved one. (Or any other calming exercise you enjoy.)
- In whatever form you choose to connect to the higher states of consciousness of love, peace, and light—allow these healing energies to fill your being and overflow through you.
- For 5-20 minutes, simply bathe in peace, allowing love to fill your cells and illuminate any areas of darkness, fatigue, disconnection, sadness, anxiety, or pain within you.
- **Let the healing presence of light strengthen, take root, and blossom within you.**
- Feel how love and peace are ever-present states of being … and over time, begin to see if you can feel how they are equally inseparable from who you really are.
- Practice connecting to and embodying these higher levels of consciousness each day, so that you can begin to carry love, joy, lightness, and peace within you more naturally as you go about your busy life.

- Practice knowing what peace and serenity feel like within you—so that you can teach your body how to connect to love even when you are sad, anxious, or overwhelmed.

  (**Please keep in mind** *you are being productive* **by taking 5-20 minutes each day to do this**. In contrast, hastily and robotically moving through your day is not being more productive. Rushing through your life while being disconnected from yourself can burn you out and rob you of your health, wisdom, and joy in life. Yes, it takes time and practice to strengthen your inner-connection muscle, but doing so will teach your mind and body how it is possible to be calm even in a chaotic world. So please know that you are *being productive* when you take a break from your busy schedule to connect inward and fill up with healing energy.)

Part 3: Walking with Grace

Mindfulness Practice #1: Commuting

When you are driving or commuting on public transportation … connect to your inner-observer and notice how you are relating to your experience of getting from one place to another.

Are you feeling rushed or annoyed while commuting?

Do you feel calm or do you feel anxious?

Is your mind thinking productively or is it defaulting into stress?

Are you feeling guilty or are you being compassionate toward yourself?

Just notice what you notice without judgment.

If you are feeling a sense of urgency or tension, gently remind yourself that you won't get to your destination any faster by being stressed out, but it will drain your energy and make your journey unnecessarily strenuous. Instead, choose to take a break from being tense or disconnected and see if you can find ease and possibly even joy in your experience.

To calm yourself down, take a deep breath in and exhale coming into the present moment and into your body.

Next, use your intention and focus to make an inner connection to the ever-present states of peace and love within you.

> (*To do so, remember what it felt like to embody peace when you were light bathing or when you were focused on nature or a loved one.* Once you have been practicing these inner-connection exercises for 5-20 minutes each day, your nervous system will be strengthening its ability to connect to these higher states of consciousness simply through using your focus and intention. This is similar to when you first learned how to walk. It took a few months to practice and learn how to it, but now you can walk simply by using your intention and desire to do so.)

Take another deep breath in and exhale. Slowly say to yourself:

I am calm.   My mind is calm.   My body is calm.

As you stay alert and fully aware as you drive …

Connect to and feel the presence of your inner-observer.

Notice the spaciousness of the deeper presence within you.

Allow a wakefulness and vibrancy to fill you.

(Even if it is subtle.)

Be the observer.

Be the witnessing awareness of consciousness itself.

Be timeless while in time.

Allow peace and lightness to expand within you.

Allow yourself to enjoy the calming, loving presence of your Soul.

After a few minutes of enjoying the spiritual presence within you gently ask yourself:

> *How would I like to experience the rest of my journey?*
>
> *Would I like to put on my favorite song, think about what I am grateful for, notice the color of the sky, listen to an audio book, practice conscious breathing, call someone I love, or simply enjoy the ride?*

As you anchor into grace, take pleasure in the rest of your journey as inner peace, stillness, and lightness blossom and expand within you.

Mindfulness Practice #2: Shopping at the grocery store

When you enter the store or walk through the aisles … take a moment to notice the energy and vibe around you.

Is it busy?

Do the other patrons seem uptight or stressed out?

Do they seem to be at ease or are they a bit frenetic?

If the energy around you doesn't feel good — simply pull your senses or your 'emotional feelers' away from them by drawing your energy closer into your body.

What exactly do I mean by drawing your energy closer into your body?

All living things have an electromagnetic field and your energy field can tune into the moods and emotions of people around you. (This is how you're able to pick up people's emotions from across the room.)

To avoid picking up energy that is not yours, draw your energy field inward about 1-2 feet around you using your intention. You can do this by visualizing your energy field in the shape of an egg. (As seen in the images below.)

Trust your ability to do this.

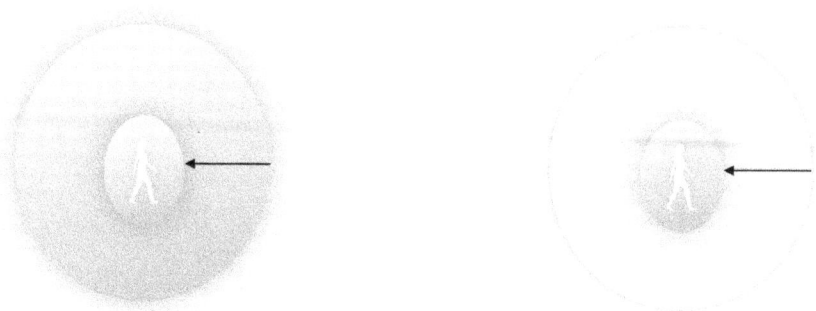

(For more support on how you can use your intention to draw your energy field in - you can watch a free coaching video on my website at belladodds.com/resources)

The next step is to create an energetic boundary.

To do this, visualize a silver light around your egg. This silver energy acts like a mirror that reflects off mental and emotional stress that is not yours.

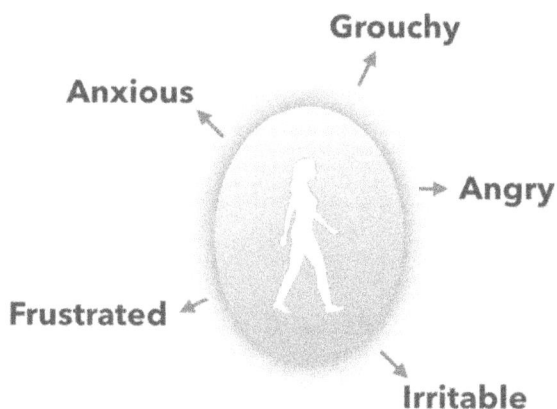

Next, you want to anchor into peace.

You can do this with your intention, or if you need more support you can visualize a calming golden light flowing into your egg.

Notice and feel how this beautiful, golden light is peaceful and soothing.

Breathe this golden light into your body and say to yourself:

I am calm. I am safe. In this moment all is well. I am unconditionally loved.

Emotions

Moods

Peace

Stress

Tension

Now glide through the aisles, filling up with peace inside yourself.

Enjoy the lightness within you as you go about the simple task of shopping.

As you check out at the register, be present and kind with the cashier. Say hello, ask how she is doing, and genuinely be interested in caring about his response. See the light and Soul behind her eyes.

Enjoy the value of this genuine exchange of kindness.

Experience the radiance in being awake and connected.

When you leave the store, notice if you feel more calm and connected than you did before you first began shopping.

Mindfulness Practice #3: Being around a loved one who is in a bad mood

If you are around a loved one, colleague, or a group of people who are in a bad mood, you can utilize the same energetic boundary technique above.

First, pull your feelers and energy away from the person or people around you who are in a bad mood. Give people space to be where they are at, as their emotions don't always need to negatively impact you or determine how you feel. After you pull your energy field in about 1-2 feet around you, put silver around your egg, and fill this inner-sanctuary with a golden light (or any luminous color that feels calming and serene to you).

After you create an energetic boundary you can say to yourself:

> *It is okay if my loved ones are in a bad mood. That's normal. Humans have ups and downs throughout the day. I am not responsible for everyone to always be in a good mood. Their*

mood is their responsibility. I am responsible for how I feel. Right now I choose to feel safe and loved inside myself. I choose to connect to peace. I choose to let the lightness and healing presence of love expand within me.

Then practice connecting to peace and getting your survival needs met on a higher level.

Visualize your egg being filled with light as you consciously slow your breathing down and connect to love. Allow your nervous system to relax. Allow yourself to feel good even if others around you are in an unpleasant mood.

Once you feel more calm and at ease you can ask yourself:

Do I want to take time to rest, go outside, or do something uplifting? What would feel nourishing and rejuvenating for me to do right now?

Or do I have a responsibility that requires my full attention? What would feel great to accomplish right now?

After tuning in with yourself and listening to your intuition on what action to take, from here, stay connected to the presence of your Soul as you *Do from Being*.

For more exercises on how to connect to peace as you go about your busy day-to-day such as:

- Learning a three-minute calming exercise
- Breathing exercises to stimulate the healthy function of your vagus nerve
- Transforming your limiting beliefs

- Empowering your inner-dialogue
- Deepening your experience of unconditional love
- Learning Primordial Sound Meditation techniques
- Creating an achievable to-do list that you can actually accomplish each day
- Finding the higher lesson amidst a conflict in a relationship
- And more …

Go to belladodds.com/resources for these free supportive coaching videos and additional techniques supporting how you can anchor into grace.

In the next chapter, we will do a deep dive into exploring various ways of how you can be strong, full, and connected within (as up to this point, we have only explored exercises that are quiet and passive). The good news is there are infinite ways to connect that are also active, creative, and adventurous.

Connecting to spiritual energy can open the door for grace to flow into your life in beautiful and unexpected ways.

While doing the final edits on this section, two clients whom I had not worked with in almost a year scheduled an appointment with me in the same week. In their sessions, both women happened to bring up their initial resistance when we'd first started working together in talking about love, peace, and spiritual energy. Given the synchronicity of their sessions, I felt called upon to share their meaningful reflections with you here.

On an early winter morning, one of my clients laughed and remarked,

> "Bella, do you remember when we first started working together how uncomfortable I was when you talked about unconditional love? It made me squirmy. I was the type of person who worked hard and got things done. Spirituality was probably twentieth on my list of what I was interested in or cared about. And now, a year later, it is one of the most important things guiding my life."

This client was a former CEO of a company that was struggling when she first took on the position, but with her innovation and leadership skills, she was able to turn it right side up and double the company's revenue within a few years. When we started working together, she was ready to move on to a new endeavor, but she wasn't sure what project she wanted to take on next. Through the coaching work we did together, her path led her toward making the choice to take a break after working diligently for so many years and to give herself time to explore meditation, healing, and conscious awareness practices.

> "After this year, I'm feeling guided to contribute my skills towards health, wellness, and longevity. I've had great opportunities come my way and different offers, but I want to make this decision based on what matters to me. I'm still not sure what it will be, but I know it needs to be something I deeply care about ..."

Two days later, in the late afternoon another client laughed and remarked in our session,

> "Do you remember how resistant I was talking about spirituality when we first started working together? After

everything that had happened in my childhood and my painful experiences around religion, it made me extremely reticent to talk about the subject. How humorous is it that now spirituality is one of the things I care about the most and I am getting my Masters Degree in Theological Studies with a focus on social justice and ethics? I didn't realize it before, but without spirituality in my life, I felt like a cut flower without any nourishment."

This client is currently a CEO and lawyer who has successfully risen out of childhood financial hardships to become highly successful in her career. Early on in working together, she expressed pain around not having done more with her law degree to fight for social justice and equality, which made it all the more beautiful to see this come full circle for her …

"In my classes, I have explored how to bring spiritual values back into policymaking. Not the current level of religion we see in politics, but the true moral values of human rights and well-being. Right now, we are operating on such hollow policies."

These two amazing and inspiring women are in the exploration stages of what they are feeling called upon to do next … yet they are trusting their intuition and allowing the wisdom of life to guide them. They are no longer influenced by making decisions based on society's pressures and values. Instead, they are connected to love. They are listening, they are awake, and they are being guided by a wise presence on how to share their skills in a way that will not only infuse deeper meaning and purpose into their own lives, but will also use their talents in ways that can uplift and strengthen others.

A week later, another client contacted me for an emergency

session. Her mother had passed away at the beginning of the pandemic, and now her brother had contracted the coronavirus and was in a coma hooked up to a ventilator and fighting for his life in the ICU. When she reached out to me for a session, her husband had just broken his leg and both his aunt and uncle had died of covid the previous week.

This amazing woman, whom I've been blessed to work with, had previously struggled with severe daily panic attacks and hypochondria, but now as I listened to her share all that she was enduring, I was humbled by her strength and steadiness. Yes, she was going through it. Yes, she was in pain and overwhelmed, but she was a different woman than she had been. Even though the worst was actually happening, she had a deeper level of faith in the process of life, and she was able to get through this crisis without being destroyed by it. Instead of becoming immobilized by panic attacks (as would've happened in the past), she deepened into her spiritual practice, she grew closer with her husband and her family, and together on a daily basis, they called on prayer to help her brother. To the doctors' surprise, her brother's once stark and unpromising prognosis began to make a miraculous turn and he came out of his coma.

For decades many of us have carried the weight of our responsibilities and challenges solely on our own shoulders, never realizing it doesn't have to all be up to us. We don't have to do it all on our own. We often put so much of our focus, time, and energy into the tangible, physical side of life without realizing that it is the invisible, formless presence within that can help aid us in ways we greatly need the support.

Love and peace are ever-present.

You can rely on these beautiful energies to give you strength.

You can rely on them to enlighten you with inspiring solutions.

You can rely on them to replenish your heart, mind, body, and spirit.

You can rely on them to comfort you when you are in pain and when all feels lost.

You can rely on them to fill you with joy and optimism, even when you are enduring great challenges.

Love and peace can bring life back into your life, color back into color, and warmth back into your heart.

They can fill what is missing in your life, and expand and overflow through you when you are empty and depleted.

They can give you the courage to be vulnerable, to stick with tough conversations, and to share deep connections with the people you love.

Peace can teach you how to enjoy your moment-to-moment experiences with richness and depth and how to feel the radiance of life even in the simplest moments.

And love can teach you how to live with your whole heart and from the level of your Soul.

In summary

When we can choose to become the observer, to slow our minds down, to surrender our stress, to let go of our current inner-dialogue, and to connect to peace within … we can get our survival needs met on a higher level. In so doing, we can feel a loving, calm, wise, beautiful, luminous presence fill and expand within us. Doing so brings grace, richness, meaning, joy, and serenity into our typical day-to-day experience (and supports us to self-heal our overactive survival stress response).

If you're at all familiar with mindfulness, it's probably safe to say that what you've learned in this chapter are concepts you've most likely heard of before; **however, in the next chapter, we're going to do something that you have probably not yet done.** I can't overstate enough the importance of being full, connected, and strong within. It is ESSENTIAL if you want to stop living in relentless stress and experience a higher quality of life and health on all levels.

Having said that, how then can you track how full and connected you are when peace and love are invisible, formless energies? In the next chapter, you are going to learn a simple yet essential technique about how to measure the invisible and quantify the formless. What exactly does that mean? You'll find out shortly.

Additionally, you are a complex human being with varying moods and energy levels each day; consequently, you need numerous ways to be connected, full, and strong within. So far, we've only explored how you can connect in focused, quiet ways ... however, there are infinite ways to be connected. In the next chapter, you are going to learn how to connect to love and peace that includes movement, laughter, friends, hobbies, fun adventures, etc.

Therefore, in our quest to work in harmony with the higher wisdom within you, the next questions we want to ask are:

How can I monitor how full and connected I am each day?

How can I keep my inner-tank full outside of mindfulness practices?

How can I strengthen my connection to love, peace, and joy in ways that are light-hearted, fun, freeing, and easy to do?

The next chapter is one of my favorites and is equally one of the most important components in the *Anchoring into Grace Method*.

You're doing great so far! Keep up the good work.

See you in Chapter 10!

10

How can I monitor how full and connected I am each day? How can I keep my inner-tank full outside of mindfulness practices? How can I strengthen my connection to love, peace, and joy in ways that are light-hearted, fun, freeing, and easy to do?

The mysterious, formless energy that gave rise to the physical universe is within all things; therefore, you can connect to love, peace, and joy in infinite and creative ways.

And you need to.

Life can be tricky and tedious at times but connecting to peace and love is the opposite ... it is a reprieve from the pressures of the world.

The good news is there is no one right way to connect.

You can connect through spiritual practices like meditation, going to church, being mindful, praying, doing yoga, etc., but you can also connect through a wide variety of healthy activities ... like laughing with friends, resting on your couch for twenty minutes guilt-free, or taking an epsom salt bath with essential oils. You can fill up with peace through painting or gardening, going on a bike ride, making love, dancing and listening to music, cooking a fun meal, walking on the beach, giving someone a hug, or reading an inspiring book.

How you connect and nourish your inner well-being is unique for you.

There is no one right way to do it—*it's just important that you take the time to do it*.

In this chapter, we are going to do a deep dive on assessing how connected you are with love, presence, and joy each day—so that you can stay strong and full on the inside—amidst the daily ups and downs of life.

First, let's look at how to take a daily self-assessment to gauge how connected you are.

Step 7: How Connected and Full Am I?

Directions:

1. Give yourself 8-10 minutes to complete this exercise.
2. To make this exercise more clear and supportive, I have provided a free audio to guide you through it at: bella-dodds.com/peace
3. Trust your intuition in this exercise. You probably haven't been asked these questions before, but that doesn't mean you don't intuitively know the answers.

Part 1: Do a self-assessment and quantify the invisible.

Quantify the invisible means that you want to you take a self-assessment to check in with yourself and see how connected and full you are. Love, peace, joy, inner-worth, and confidence are invisible states of being—so in order to make yourself conscious of where you are on a daily basis—I have developed a simple exercise to measure how connected you are in a *visible, tangible, and practical way*.

To be guided through the exercise, you can listen to it at belladodds.com/peace

Okay, get into a comfortable position and take a nice deep breath in ...

And gently close your eyes.

Today you want to check in with yourself and measure how full and connected you are.

First, tune into your inner awareness.

Notice how you feel in your body.

Now notice the energy of the room you are in.

Become aware that your senses actually extend a bit beyond your physical body and that your senses do not stop at the surface of your skin. (This is how you are able to sense the moods and emotions of people around you, even if they are on the other side of the room.)

In recognizing this, I'd like you to connect with your inner-awareness as being in the shape of an egg about 2-3 feet around your body.

Trust your ability to sense this.

Think of this egg as a container and you are going to measure how full or empty your container is.

In the previous chapters, you practiced connecting with love and peace through nature, an animal, a person, or through light bathing.

From those exercises, please reflect on which focus point felt the most natural and easy for you to use. In other words, which focus created the strongest feeling of peace or love within you? Nature, an animal, a person, or light? Even if it was a subtle sensation of relaxation, please pick the focus that was most natural for you and created the strongest connection.

Okay, great. Now I would like you to gently think of either that place in nature, an animal, a person, or light.

In your inner awareness, go to your favorite place in nature, be with the Soul you love, or feel light flowing into your body.

Be there now.

Gently allow the warmth of peace and love to fill inside you.

Let it feel good.

Breathe in the lightness and let it expand.

Breathe in the peace.

Breathe in the love.

Let peace and love expand inside you.

Now, in this moment, gently notice do you feel empty or do you feel full?

On a scale of 0-100% (0% being completely empty and 100% being totally full):

How full do you feel? How full is your egg?

How connected do you feel on a scale of 0-100%?

How full do you feel with a sense of love for yourself on a scale of 0-100%?

Trust your intuition.

Do you feel 30%, 50%, 80% full? Do you feel 100% full?

Just notice what you notice. There is no right or wrong answer.

Trust your intuition.

Okay, gently open your eyes and write down your answers from this exercise:

> On a scale of 0-100%—how full do you feel?
>
> On a scale of 0-100%—how connected are you?
>
> On a scale of 0-100%—how full do you feel with a sense of love for yourself?

Part 2: Take a self-assessment based on your average day

Before reading *Anchoring into Grace*, how full and connected were you to peace and love on average each day? Meaning, before learning this material, how full and connected were you on a daily basis on a scale of 0-100%? Remember, we're trying to make the invisible—measurable.

Please fill in the ovals below to make your self-assessment visible, tangible, and trackable: (If you were 10% full draw a line in the lower quadrant that reflects the oval being 10% full.)

How full and connected did I feel with peace, love, or a spiritual energy of my own understanding?	How full and connected did I feel with love for myself?
⬭	⬭

Coaching Note: On average, most of my clients assessed that they were around 5-20% connected and full each day. This is normal due to so much of our modern-day society's focus on the outer world. The good news is, you can begin to fill up and be stronger on the inside within days and weeks as you tend to your inner world and take time each day for things that connect, strengthen, and fill you with a sense of serenity, relaxation, and joy.

* If you'd like to print out this worksheet and track how connected you are each week, there is a free PDF of this exercise at belladodds.com/peace

Part 3: How full and connected do you WANT to feel on average each day?

In order to enjoy your life more and feel more calm, how full and connected with love and peace do you want to be each day?

In other words, right now if you are averaging being 10% full, you are most likely burnt-out and probably don't feel so great.

With that said, how much better would you feel if you were 50% full and connected each day?

Please trust your intuition and pick a percentage that you want to *begin to work with over the next month*. Know that there is an exponential difference in how much better you will feel going from 10% to 50% full.

How full & connected do I want to be on average?	How full & connected do I want to feel each day with love for myself?

Coaching Note: Please set yourself up to succeed by intuitively working with an achievable goal of how full and connected you want to be this month. For example, wanting to be 95-100% full when you've been running on empty, is a bit unrealistic considering how challenging the world can be. Yet, going from 20% full to 60% full will make a life-changing difference, as you will soon experience when you apply this to your own life.

What do I mean by: *How full and connected do I want to feel each day with love for myself?*

You have probably heard the importance of loving yourself or of practicing self-love and self-care. Over the years, what I have found to be most effective in assisting my clients to authentically love themselves, is to encourage them to make a direct connection to a spiritual energy of their own understanding (Love, Peace, Source, God, Allah, Brahman, Jesus, the Universe, Great Spirit, the Divine, etc.). Over time as my clients connect with these healing energies, they naturally begin to feel their inherent worth and love themselves through osmosis, and with far less inner struggle or questioning if they are truly worthy of love.

When you directly connect to spiritual energy, you will begin to feel the beautiful presence of love within you and you can discover that love is inseparable from who you really are. From here, you will no longer need to practice loving yourself or trying to be worthy of love—instead you can practice connecting to the *state of being of love.* Over time you can begin to know that you are made of love and that you are beautiful, whole, complete, and perfect just as you are. And as you practice filling up with love each day, it will become easier and more natural for you to connect (even when you are anxious or overwhelmed). With practice, you will be able to move through your day with the presence of love within you, and with grace, you can naturally begin to love yourself authentically.

Therefore, the question: How full do you want to feel with a sense of love for yourself?

If you previously felt 10% full and connected with love for yourself, how much better would you feel, and how much more confident would you be if you were moving through your day feeling 50% full with love for yourself?

Intuitively, pick an amount that you would like to work with over the next month.

(You may want to try working with being 50% full this first month, and 60% full the next month.)

If you found reading through this exercise confusing in anyway, I encourage you to listen to the free audio as being guided through this process should help bring clarity. If you are still confused, you can leave me a comment on my Facebook or Instagram page, and if my schedule and time allows, I will clarify questions you may have.

You can connect with me at:

Facebook: @HigherMindHealth
Instagram: @belladodds

I post on a regular basis on these platforms sharing inspiring perspectives, calming meditations, breathing exercises, and various tools to help you process your challenges on a higher level. I would love to connect with you and have you be a part of a community that values spiritual growth, courage, kindness, healing, and joy.

How can I connect and fill up with peace, love, and joy each day and in ways that are practical, fun, freeing, and easy to do?

In the next step, Step 8, you are going to come up with a list of activities that help you to replenish yourself when you have low energy days, when you have high energy days, as well as for when you are limited on time.

In creating your list, you will explore things that light you up, make you feel good, inspire you, as well as activities that can calm your mind and body down. Now this might be easy for you to do, or it might seem like a daunting task.

If the notion of creating a list of what makes you happy is stressful in any way … please know that's okay!

Actually, it's normal.

Why?

Well, if you've been overly responsible trying to hold everything together and overworking yourself for decades, then it is quite possible that you don't really know what makes you happy anymore …

Take my client Luz, for example.

Luz had no idea what made her happy as she'd spent her whole life taking care of her alcoholic parents and she did so well into her late 30s. It wasn't until both of her parents passed away that she experienced a huge void in her life and realized that she didn't know who she was outside of being a responsible caretaker.

Beautifully, this amazing woman with a heart of gold redirected the energy she had been giving away to everyone else, and she re-channeled some of it into exploring, experimenting, and discovering what brought her joy, what made her feel good, and what nourished her Soul. As part of her self-discovery, Luz let go of any preconceived judgments that she wouldn't like something, and instead, she let herself explore and experiment whether she liked an activity or not.

Luz tried taking art classes, dance classes, and online classes. She began experimenting with cooking, reading books on spirituality, and traveling. She tried standup paddling and sailing, she explored various exercise programs, she dated, she went to Al-anon and Adult Children of Alcoholics meetings … and she practiced saying no.

So, if you're like Luz, and you don't know what brings you joy or makes you feel good, that's 100% okay! Discovering what makes you feel alive, what fills you with confidence, what brings you peace and inner tranquility is actually an important and sacred part of your healing journey. (You're also about to have a lot more fun in life by discovering what nourishes you on a Soul level.)

If you are reading *Anchoring into Grace* during the pandemic—or if you have a hectic schedule and are short on options for doing activities that bring you joy—it's time to get creative.

Love, joy, and peace are a choice. These higher states of consciousness are ever-present and available to you at all times. Your job is to strengthen your ability to connect to them and feel their lightness within you, even when life around you is intense and tedious. Especially during challenging times, we must learn to take breaks and pull away from all of the hardships, pressures, and negativity of the world and CHOOSE to connect inward and ask:

What do I need?

What would help connect me to peace and love right now?

What would strengthen me?

Do I need to rest?

Do I need to do something fun and energizing?

I'll give you one example from my own life of how I connected to joy during the pandemic. For years now, I've been going to my hip-hop cardio dance class several times a week at my local gym. I love to dance and I love my dance community. Together we dance out our stress, we get out of our heads, and we find our joy together through movement, laughter, and music.

During the pandemic, I knew I still needed to have this healing medicine in my life and that I needed to find it in a new, reliable way where I could feel supported and nourished on a weekly basis. YouTube has been my go-to for finding great hip-hop teachers, HIIT cardio, and strength training classes; however, the best was when I unexpectedly stumbled onto Buti Yoga. Buti combines yoga, belly dancing, hip-hop, HIIT cardio, shaking, stretching, and moving in spiral patterns. I love the diversity of switching from cardio, to stretching, to strength training, to twerking, to child's pose, to dancing. I love the intensity, how playful it is while also breaking free from rigid, boxed-in, predictable movements.

When the pandemic hit, I knew I needed to bring joy into my daily life—and I knew that it was my responsibility to do this. Finding Buti has been an inspiring new addition to my health and wellness plan, along with finding many other great workout classes on YouTube. The virus was not in my control, but finding my peace, love, joy, and health is and always will be my responsibility. I don't have total control over the outer world, but I do have control over finding time to connect and be strong within. So with that said, coming up with your list will take a bit more creativity if you're reading this during the pandemic or if you have a hectic schedule, but I also know…

"Within every problem that we face, there is always a solution to take its place!"

(A li'l line from my children's book, *The Butterfly Story*.)

Embrace the adversity of this moment. Empower yourself and focus on what you *can* control and get creative as you come up with your list—because if you want to feel good—you need to do things that make you feel good.

If you want to feel peaceful—you need to do things that teach your nervous system how to relax and feel calm.

If you want to feel confident and love yourself—you need to do things that connect you to the presence of love within you.

If you want others to love you unconditionally—then you need to feel how you are already unconditionally loved—and you need to love yourself unconditionally too.

If you want to enjoy your life—then you need to do things that bring you joy on a regular basis.

If you want to be light-hearted and more present with your family—you need to take time for yourself to be full on the inside—so that you can be more patient, easy-going, and loving with them.

If you want to self-heal and change your life—you need to schedule in non-negotiable, self-care time—and do so 100% guilt-free.

If you want to stop living in survival mode—then you need to teach your nervous system how to connect to an ocean of peace inside you.

To help get you going on creating your list, here are few activities that scientific studies have shown to boost serotonin, oxytocin, endorphins, and dopamine in your body. These hormones are often referred to as the 'Happy Hormones' as they make you feel good, calm, confident, energized, and uplifted.

Serotonin - The Joyful Hormone
Walking in nature or in a park
Exercising (dancing, swimming, cycling, etc.)
Yoga
Meditation
Massage/acupuncture
Being grateful
Spending time in the sun
If you live in a climate with infrequent sunny days, sitting in front of a SAD lamp for 20 minutes a day can support healthier serotonin levels. (I lived in London for a year. Please don't hesitate to get a SAD lamp. They can help a great deal!)

- *Low levels of serotonin are linked to: anxiety, depression, fatigue, insomnia, lack of mental clarity and reasoning, weight gain, addictions, migraines, a lower threshold for physical pain.*

- *Balanced levels of serotonin are linked to: decreased cravings for sugars and carbohydrates, an increase in happiness, and an over-all feeling of well-being.*

Oxytocin - The Love Chemical
Giving a compliment, being kind, doing something for others
Listening and being present
Physical touch (holding hands and hugging people you love)

Playing with animals
Cuddling, kissing, sex, or flying solo!
Volunteering or being kind to a stranger
Smiling and laughing
Expressing emotions/crying
Practicing compassion and empathy
Sunlight exposure
Taking an epsom salt bath

- *Low levels of oxytocin are linked to:* decreased levels of trust and emotional bonding, poor communication, fear of social betrayal, isolation, less desire to socialize.

- *Balanced levels of oxytocin are linked to:* increasing your trust in social interactions and interest in social activities, being less sensitive to other's moods and subtle social cues, decreased fear of being betrayed socially, and decreasing cortisol levels in your body.

Endorphin - The Pain Killer
Laughing at least once a day (try watching a comedy)
Singing
Stretching (just a few minutes can help invigorate you and boost your endorphin levels)
Volunteering or helping others
Exercise
Listening to music
Playing with a child or pet
Breathing exercises
Being in nature/going on a walk in the park
Tai Chi

- *Low levels of endorphins are linked to:* an increase in physical pain, sensitivity to pain, increase in moodiness, depression, anxiety.

- *Balanced levels of oxytocin are linked to:* pain relief (studies show endorphin molecules are up to 33 times stronger than morphine), block pain receptors, improve sleep, an increase in happiness, higher self-esteem, and a desire for social interaction, as well as helping to regulate appetite, improve weight loss, and boost the body's immune system.

Dopamine - The Motivation Chemical
Listening to music that is inspiring or calming
Breathing exercises
Journaling
Listening to an inspiring podcast
Exercise
Meditation apps
Completing a task/celebrating little wins
Eating healthy food
Healing/coaching work
Being grateful
Artistic exploration such as: arts and crafts, playing an instrument, writing, reading poetry.
Cold showers/cold plunges

> (I love doing cold plunges in mountain lakes and frigid rivers. I breathe and settle into a deep, blissful stillness. Afterwards, I'm rewarded with feeling invigorated, as well as enjoying the health benefits that come with decreasing inflammation throughout my body and sleeping like a baby that evening. If you'd like to give cold showers a try, there is an article in the

Reference section that can guide you on how to ease into taking them.)

- *Low levels of dopamine are linked to: a lack of vitality, drive, motivation, concentration, memory, focus, critical thinking, and creativity. Studies also show an increase in depression, laziness, lethargy, difficulty in completing tasks, and making decisions.*

- *Balanced levels of dopamine are linked to: increased motivation, improving your quality of sleep, increasing your sex drive, improving your mental clarity and focus, and decreasing anxiety and depression.*

If you'd like to learn more about the different ways you can naturally boost 'Happy Hormones' in your body, I've listed several articles you can check out in the Reference section. This is an empowering area of research and I'd encourage you to dive in deeper (as I've only shared a brief introduction here). If you prefer academic articles, I recommend the *US National Library of Medicine and National Institutes of Health.* Their website is: https://www.ncbi.nlm.nih.gov/. If you prefer quick, easy-to-read articles, I recommend both goodtherapy.org and bebrainfit.com.

Ironically, I only recently came across this research but I'm grateful I did. Not only do I find it inspiring to incorporate into my own life, but I am equally thankful for how it brings scientific backing to the work I've been doing with my clients for years. It may sound simplistic, but I have witnessed **massive changes in my clients' mental, emotional, physical, and spiritual well-being simply by them consciously pulling back on trying to do the impossible and simultaneously replacing**

old behaviors with taking more time for what brings joy into their lives.

When you STOP disconnecting from yourself and giving 95% of your energy away to the outer world, and you START being connected and strong within, you will not only feel better, but you will also begin to reverse your overactive survival stress response. How so? When you are well-resourced and centered within, you will be like a strong oak tree with deep roots into the Earth. When a storm comes, you can bend, but you will not break. You will be less reactive and more responsive. And instead of being triggered fifty times a day living at the end of your rope, you may only be triggered a few times a day (which is normal—and you will discover in chapter 11 that these triggers are healthy opportunities for you to evolve, heal, and grow).

Okay, let's get to it and come up with your list of things that bring you joy, make you feel good, nourish, and replenish you!

Step 8: Fill Up and Connect to Peace, Love, and Joy Every day

Directions:

1. Give yourself 10 minutes to complete this exercise.
2. Get creative and go beyond the obvious with which activities could bring you joy, connect you to yourself, light you up, feed your Soul, nourish you, calm you, center you, and reunite you with your Source.
3. Give yourself permission to explore and play.

You'll see a two-column tier below: one side is for days when you are feeling more quiet, tired, and introverted, and the other is for days when you are feeling energized and extroverted.

Now set a timer and give yourself 10 minutes to get creative.

Why a timer?

When I ask my clients to do this exercise, the majority take less than a minute and list five things they know they already like and then say to me, "That's it. I can't think of any more."

To which my response is, "We're talking about your ability to enjoy your life and feel better! That's it? That's all you've got?"

We laugh (because healing work does not need to be heavy), and then I lovingly invite them to go deeper and think a bit harder, and pretty soon they've got an inspiring list going. As they come up with more ideas, I can hear a sense of excitement in their voice, as well as relief that part of their healing journey is to make fun, tranquility, and joy an essential part of their everyday lives.

So please dig deep and get creative.

Now set your timer, and here are a few questions to open up your intuition …

Part 1: Questions to open up your intuition and create your list:

What do I like to do for fun? What hobbies do I enjoy?
What makes me laugh?
What healthy activities make me feel good or happy?
What healthy activities help me feel alive and energized?
What brings me peace or calms my mind and body down?
What connects me to Love, God, Spirit, or the Universe?

What activities or hobbies connect me to myself and help me to feel more confident?

What practices help me to connect to stillness and be in the present moment?

What subjects inspire me?

What lights up my Soul?

What brought me joy when I was younger? Did I play an instrument? Did I sing? Did I play a sport?

What do I want to learn, or what skill do I want to get better at?

What are my simple pleasures?

What do I enjoy doing by myself?

What do I enjoy doing with others?

On the next page, I will give you several creative examples from my clients to help you with a few more ideas, but first, connect with yourself and practice going within to explore the answers to these personal questions.

YIN (quiet, introverted, gentle energy)	YANG (active, social, outside energy)

Examples from clients:

YIN (quiet, gentle, introverted, energy)	YANG (active, social, outside energy)
Plant flowers or a vegetable garden	Go on a walk
Spend time in nature	Hike
Make chocolate truffles low in sugar	Ski
Lie in the sun for 20-60 mins	Dance
Lie on the couch & connect to love	Go out to dinner with friends
Talk to a friend on the phone	Play an instrument
Meditate/listen to a guided meditation	Go to church or to a temple
Read a book/listen to an audiobook	Hike to a mountain stream
Cuddle/sex/have orgasms	Go to the beach
Take a bath with essential oils	Go bowling
Study an inspiring subject	Have a game night with my family
Listen to Ted Talks	Take a spin class
Take an online Yin Yoga class	Go on a trip & fun adventure
Pray or read spiritual texts	Take an acting or improv class
Pick cards in a spiritual deck	Take a pottery or sculpting class
Make a special meal (don't rush)	Go to a bookstore or coffee shop
Bake & watch a fun movie while cooking	Go stand up paddling
Listen & sing to music	Plan a camping trip
Get a massage or actupuncture	Go golfing
Take a lunch break & enjoy it (without multi-tasking)	Play volleyball, soccer, basketball, badminton
Play cards or do puzzles	Go on a meditation retreat
Stargaze	Go skydiving
Journal	Take a water aerobics class
Learn how to knit	Take a cooking class
Feng shui house	Go on a spontaneous adventure
Learn a new language	Volunteer for a cause

Great job on completing Step 8!

Now it is important to pull all of this together and start practicing two basic concepts each day:

1. Check in with yourself to assess how full and connected you are.
2. Make time to connect and fill up with Soul replenishing self-care each day.

(Below is a worksheet you can use to check in with yourself 2-3 times a day.)

Morning

How am I feeling right now? On a scale of 0%-100% — how full and connected am I?

How full do I feel with love for myself?

What can I do to connect and fill up with peaceful or uplifting energy before I start my day?

Do I want to do something calming, centering, or energizing?

Mid-Day

How am I feeling right now? On a scale of 0%-100% — how full and connected am I?

How full do I feel with a sense of love for myself?

What can I do to connect and refuel for the second half of today?

Do I want to do something relaxing, rejuvenating, or energizing?

Evening

How am I feeling right now? On a scale of 0%-100% — how connected am I?

How full do I feel with spiritual energy?

What can I do to connect to peace? What am I grateful for? How can I strengthen my trust and faith in life before I go to bed?

Coaching Notes: When you are strengthening your ability to be connected during your day—please keep in the front of your mind—this does not mean you have to feel happy, peaceful, and joyful all day long. Instead, being connected is about learning how to check in with yourself and monitor how full your tank is on a regular basis. Doing so will help you to avoid running on empty and replace burnout with being more energized, resilient, confident, loving, and optimistic.

If you're feeling heavy, sad, anxious, or depleted, it can be hard to know what you need in that moment—that's when you definitely want to look at your Yin Yang list. Your pre-made list will support you with what nourishing actions you can take to help you get centered, grounded, connected, and uplifted. **Remember, you don't always need an hour in order to feel better. Sometimes it is one small step out of overwhelm towards inner peace that can make a world of difference.** You can simply lie on the couch with an ice pack on your forehead for 10 minutes (guilt-free) and take deep breaths while listening to a guided meditation. (The app, the *Insight*

Timer, is a great resource with hundreds of free meditations to choose from.)

Just remember, it doesn't have to be complicated. When you take a few minutes to slow your brainwaves down, take space from your obstacle, and reset yourself—a simple mini-break can make all the difference in helping you to find your center and elevate your perspective. One day you might want to meditate, the next, you might feel lethargic or sad and need to take a walk outside to uplift your mood. Tune in and ask your intuition what you need—and just know that the more you ask yourself what you need—**the stronger your intuition will become**.

If you go a few days or weeks forgetting to connect and fill up—please don't beat yourself up about it.

After practicing regular self-care for a few months, you may be feeling good and suddenly get caught up with life and slip back into old behaviors of running on empty. Perhaps something comes up at work or with your family and you get swept away with an intense week. At first, skipping your self-care time may feel okay, but over time, the price you pay can be a heavy one. If you slip back to operating at 5-20% full, you will have less energy and wisdom to handle the daily ups and downs that come your way.

So just keep in mind ahead of time ... it is normal and okay to forget to connect. But once you realize you've neglected your inner well-being, the best next step is to schedule time to replenish and regenerate your energy levels as soon as possible. Gently ask yourself:

How full and connected am I right now?

What do I need to do to fill up, center myself, and feel better?

If you find yourself running on empty—be compassionate with yourself. The truth is, you've identified a key problem of being disconnected from yourself, and you can feel empowered knowing that you're taking your first steps toward getting back to your center.

If you are having an exceptionally busy week, make sure to take mini-breaks throughout the day.

Mini-breaks can make a big difference in keeping your inner tank full. If you are feeling tired and only have 10 minutes, give yourself permission to lie in the sun or on the couch and do the light bathing exercise. If you are feeling irritated and only have 15 minutes, give yourself permission to have a dance break, listen to uplifting music, talk with a friend, or get out of the house. If you only have 5 minutes, go on a mindfulness walk and give yourself a quick break to get out of your head and look up at the sky, birds, and trees and simply breathe and be. (Do this 100% guilt-free and fully take in the beauty and vibrancy of life within and around you.) Even when you don't think you have a minute to spare, you can practice anchoring into grace throughout your day. You can be mindful, breathe, flow, and feel serenity expanding within you as you: *Do from Being.*

Remember, when you are full and strong on the inside, you'll be much less likely to get knocked down or stay knocked down when life hands you an unexpected challenge. Or as a fiercely wise and ever-hilarious Soul once said,

"You are too special to ignore your needs queen!"
Jonathan Van Ness

Taking an hour or more for yourself each week is equally as vital as taking mini-breaks.

The good news is, when you work with the principles in this book, you will be able to create more time.

How?

Your survival strategies like perfectionism, people pleasing, problem-solving, being a workaholic—all take up a helluva lotta time. On your healing journey, as you begin to practice using your strengths in balanced, healthy ways, you will simultaneously be creating new windows of time for yourself.

So please pull back on saying:

> *I have too much to do. I don't have enough time for myself.*

> *I never have enough time to get everything done ... let alone to do things for myself!*

These are all self-fulfilling prophecies, but they are also reflective of living in survival mode when all of your time and energy goes into focusing on the world around you. If you find yourself saying you never have enough time, please consider changing your inner dialogue. Here are a few possible suggestions:

> *My self-care time is non-negotiable—it brings out the best in me and makes me a better person.*

> *My family benefits when I take care of myself.*

I make more money, I feel healthier, and I am more confident when I practice daily self-care.

If I want to feel good—I need to make time and do things that make me feel good.

If I want to enjoy my life—I need to do things that bring me joy.

I'm putting my phone on airplane mode—I'll get back to you in an hour!

If you are a visual person, perhaps it helps to think of being strong, connected, and full within from this perspective:

**WHEN YOU ARE FULL
YOU SPIRAL UP AND ARE:**

Joyful   Optimistic   Wise   Calm   Loving   Patient   Centered   Kind   Courageous   Strong   Resilient   Confident   Connected   Trusting   Warm

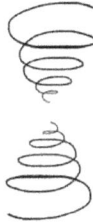

**WHEN YOU ARE EMPTY
YOU SPIRAL DOWN AND ARE:**

Overwhelmed   Burnt-out   Controlling   Critical   Judgmental   Mean   Impatient   Anxious   Depressed   Lonely   Disconnected   Dishonest   Shutdown

---

Schedule in your joy and peace.

If you have a busy schedule and know it will be difficult to make time for yourself—I'd suggest blocking out at least three hours for yourself in your calendar each week. If you make feeling good a priority, it will happen. If you don't, it probably won't.

Self-heal and make it real...

Anchor into Grace	Make Feeling Good a Priority
Monday (AM)	(PM)
Tuesday (AM)	(PM)
Wednesday (AM)	(PM)
Thursday (AM)	(PM)
Friday (AM)	(PM)
Saturday (AM)	(PM)
Sunday (AM)	(PM)

* After 2-4 weeks of making your inner peace and well-being a priority—notice if your energy levels, state of mind, optimism, and relationships have improved.

Keeping your inner tank full is not being selfish; it is being wise.

Being strong on the inside is the opposite of being selfish. If you are more centered, patient, and confident—if you are more calm, loving, compassionate, and joyful—that is who you will show up as more often in the world.

If you don't take time to be strong within, you're much more likely to show up exhausted, irritated, critical, worried, overwhelmed, judgmental, impatient, angry, anxious, or burnt-out (as well as increasing the likelihood that you will project your pain and frustration onto others).

When you feel better, you will treat the people you love better too. When you are more centered, connected, calm, and full of love on the inside, you can be more centered, connected, calm, and loving with your family. When you see your own worth and value yourself, you can more easily be able to see and value the people in your life too. When you feel the healing presence of love within you, you can be more kind to yourself and to others. It will also help you to be less judgmental with yourself and others. **When you take time for yourself, know that the world will be better for it.**

Some days will be trickier to connect than others.

Even though peace and love are one with your deepest Self, this does not mean these higher states of consciousness will always be easy to connect with. Some days will be easier to connect and some days can be trickier.

Here is an example from my own life …

During mid-August through mid-September of 2020, while writing this book, the days were hot. Fires were burning throughout the West, as well as several just miles away from where I live in Colorado. The air was red, dense, smoky, and unbreathable at times. The news was raging, I was experiencing a challenge in a relationship, and I was struggling with a difficult hurdle in writing this book.

During that month, connecting to peace wasn't as natural or as easy for me as it usually is ... but I didn't spiral out for too long. When I realized what was happening, I surrendered and leaned into my personal healing medicines. I spent more time in nature, more time with family, rested in silence, and practiced humbly accepting and embracing the challenges that were coming my way.

A key point I want you to know is that I did not put my head down and blood, sweat, and tear it or force myself to push through. I did not exhaust or deplete myself as I would have in years past. Instead I surrendered.

I surrendered and trusted that I was being presented with these challenges for a reason.

I practiced being compassionate with myself.

I practiced being compassionate with others.

I read books, I prayed, I gained insight from other coaches, and I learned invaluable insights from their suggestions.

I practiced asking myself:

> How is this helping me to mature and be prepared for what I most want in life?

Through my surrender a few answers came through ...

One in particular was that by writing this book, I was expanding farther outward, which was unconsciously pushing me past my comfort zone, and with it, new levels of protection were popping up inside of me.

I suddenly felt like an exposed soft-shell crab that had outgrown its protective shell and was scurrying around bare-skinned and disrobed.

How could I write from here?

I wanted to hide, not write.

The truth is writing is not natural for me … I do my best, but it is not my lead strength. I write because I have a Bigger Why of wanting to help people learn how to connect to the healing energy inside themselves. But my Bigger Why started to be eclipsed by my comfort zone. Suddenly, after months of writing comfortably, I felt like I had a bad sunburn, and every day as I opened my computer, it felt like I was willingly making my sunburn worse.

It may sound dramatic, but I guess that is why vulnerability can be so uncomfortable. It is hard to feel unprotected and to keep pushing that edge week after week, month after month.

Another healing insight that came through was …

If I was going to expand farther outward, then I needed to grow deeper roots into Source and to equally expand with love. Instead of pulling back into my old shell, I could let the Universe's beautiful energy fill into my expansion, and in so doing embody new levels of strength, commitment, inspiration, peace, and courage. It became clear during this time that how I was playing the game was no longer adequate, and I needed to up my commitment to connecting to love on a higher level, each day, and every day.

Was this a challenging, raw period? Yes. It was scary and uncomfortable, but it was equally beautiful and I am a better person for having gone through it. After my personal storm cleared, I felt stronger and more connected. I felt my voice strengthen. I felt clearer. I felt more like myself and my writing flowed once again. Through embracing my lessons, I was able to connect to a spiritual energy that is far greater than myself, and in doing so, make room for grace to flow into my life and support me on my journey up life's great mountain.

Humbly, I know these lessons were essential for me to learn and to become a more integrated, loving person, as well as to prepare me for the next leg of my journey and what I most want in life.

So even though I still feel raw while writing some days, I choose to share over hiding.

I choose to serve others over protecting myself.

I choose collective well-being over my personal comfort zone.

This was a long chapter, so let's sum it up!

To be strong in the world is first and foremost an inside job, and in order to be full within, you must take time to replenish your inner well-being everyday (even if some days you only can find 5-10 minutes). Fortunately, there are infinite ways to connect and fill up, and taking time to do so will bring greater joy, meaning, and peace to your life. You will also be better equipped to handle the storms and unexpected challenges that come your way when you are strong within, as well as to think more clearly. Life will have ups and downs every day, but you can counterbalance the effects of this by monitoring how full your tank is, and when you are running low, you can take non-negotiable time to restore and replenish yourself (even if that means lying on the couch light bathing for 20 minutes guilt-free). When you pull back on over-using your survival strategies and stop trying to do the impossible, and take time to be strong within yourself, you will not only feel better, but you can also begin to reverse your overactive survival stress response. From here, instead of being triggered fifty-plus times a day, you will be more calm and centered so that when a challenge does come your way … you can begin to see it as an invitation to learn and grow.

Which brings us to the last question in the *Anchoring into Grace Method:*

> *How can I embrace my challenges and have them bring out the best in me?*

Evolving out of a control mindset to a growth mindset has the ability to change your life in profound and inspiring ways.

See you in the final chapter!

11

How can I embrace my challenges and have them bring out the best in me?

Over the years, I've migrated with the humpback whales to Hawaii during the winter months to visit my dear friend Amy and spend a few weeks surfing with her on Maui. As a Colorado kid, I didn't grow up surfing, but I did learn to ski not long after I began walking. My first clear, exhilarating memory of skiing was when I was probably about four or five years old and I begged a family friend for her ski poles. When she finally relented, I took off down the bunny hill with her poles (that were almost as big as my body) tucked tightly under my arms, speeding down the mountain going faster than I'd ever gone before! (This is also one of my first vividly, clear memories in life.) Now even though I have zero recollection of my first days on skis … I still have to believe that surfing is much harder to learn than skiing.

For starters, the whole mountain isn't moving and changing at every moment. A ski run is reliable. A Green Run doesn't suddenly become a Black Diamond out of nowhere. And if you crash while you're skiing, you can lie on the mountain until you're ready to get up—you don't have to hold your breath diving under wave after wave in the crash zone. (And last I checked you aren't worried about sharks possibly swimming in the three feet of powder next to you.)

Surfing, on the other hand, exists on an entirely different level.

The ocean can change quickly and sometimes dramatically. Numerous times I've been out there paddling around, doing my best on the tiny waves, when out of nowhere, a set comes in, doubled in size, and I suddenly go from thinking, "This is doable. I'm doing good," to whispering, "*Ohhh shhhit …*" On one such incident, I tried to get out of the crash zone but to no avail and got pummeled like a rag doll in a washing machine, getting sea water up my nose, ears, and everywhere else.

Surfing is a humbling experience to say the least.

But I still love it.

In the winter of 2015, Amy's friend Stephen, a local island videographer, gave me a surf lesson in exchange for some super delicious Maui Farmer's Market banana bread. We began the lesson by sitting on the beach looking out on the ocean and watching the power, depth, and peace in front of us. We slowed our breathing and minds down and allowed the busy world on land to drift away as we tuned in and connected to the ocean's unique rhythms that morning. Before going in, Stephen shared a few gems to help me navigate the ocean as a new surfer …

> *"Can you see how the waves are coming in as sets? Typically, they come in sets of 3-7. Sometimes they come in sets of ten or more though. So if a big set does come in, remember not to panic. If things suddenly get intense and you're in the crash zone, just know that the intensity will pass …*
>
> *And keep in mind that one gallon of water weighs around eight pounds - so the ocean is always going to win - always.*

Don't fight or try to be in control. Respect the ocean, pay attention, and find your ease in her rhythms.

And remember to stay relaxed. Don't tighten up or breathe shallow - you'll wear yourself out fast doing that. Just remember to breathe with even, deep breaths, and stay open and calm.

Oh and you will definitely wipe out!

Definitely.

It's all part of being out there.

So keep the freak-out factor to a minimum.

Just remember, if you're smiling and laughing ... you're doing it right."

I think one of the reasons I love surfing so much is that it mirrors life, but on a raw, magnified scale. You're out there on a small board floating on the surface of a massive, powerful ocean as waves are coming in, picking you up, and crashing all around you. It's humbling out there. And rightfully so. It teaches you (mercilessly at times) how to find the sweet spot between humility, faith, patience ... and gumption, commitment, and digging in. How to be alert, but calm. Confident, but not cocky. Staying in your range of ability, but equally being ready to grow at any moment. Respecting others, while still being assertive. Maintaining a calm breath, even when you're scared. Feeling the intensity of being right on the edge of your comfort zone, while not retreating to the safety of the shore. But the most resounding lesson is—it eclipses any false belief that you can somehow bend the ocean to your will. Out there, you FEEL the power that is far greater than yourself, and you know your wisest choice is to surrender and let the sea teach you, moment by moment, how to navigate its magnificent force, how to be in harmony with it, and how to let it pick you up and take you on a beautiful ride.

When you live with a growth mindset, you live in harmony with the ocean of life. That is why it rewards you.

A growth mindset is fulfilling and helps you to make steady progress each day—while simultaneously supporting you to feel calm in your body, and clear and focused in your mind.

The moment you choose to grow with life (rather than resist or control it), you feel yourself shift into the present moment.

Your mind grows quiet.

You become grounded.

You feel steady.

Overwhelm is replaced by an inner mandala of courage, faith, inspiration, joy, self-assurance, love, and determination.

You feel one with your Soul and you are ready to go.

Each day life will give you the invitation to grow.

Whether you choose to grow or not is up to you.

When you are confronted with something you don't like, you have the free will to resist it, to complain that it's too hard, to shut down, to recoil and protect yourself, to feel hopeless, to blame others, to try and control the situation—**or you have the**

choice to embrace your adversity, to accept the discomfort, to take full responsibility, to connect with love, and to rise up and grow.

Fortunately, when you do choose to grow and learn the higher lessons life is seeking to teach you—not only do you open the door for grace to flow into your everyday life—you equally empower yourself to move through your lessons more quickly.

Now it is unrealistic to think that you will choose to grow every second of every day. Yet the more you practice, the more you can strengthen a new habit within yourself—and perhaps in time trust that everything is happening for your highest good—even if you can't see the higher purpose in that moment.

Here is a process I go through when I am confronted with a challenge:

> When it's clear I'm in a tough spot, I give myself permission to find time to pull away from the world and connect inward. I close my eyes, still my mind, open up and connect with the healing presence of peace and love. As I connect, I begin to feel that I am not separate from the world around me; instead, I feel a formless, expansive presence within all things. This presence is loving, alive, filled with light, and embodies an infinite wisdom. It fills me with reverence and a knowing that this beautiful light is my teacher, it is far wiser than me, and I have a great deal to learn from it.
>
> By slowing down and connecting to this higher energy, I am able to create space from my emotionally charged point of view. From here, I realize I can choose to turn away from love and let my ego rant in an endless

loop of my grievances (keeping me stuck in my frustration, pain, fear, and disappointment), or I can choose to surrender and allow love's healing light to soothe me and teach me a beautiful new perspective and understanding that I am currently not seeing.

At this point in my life, I am far less interested in holding tightly to my ego's story for days or weeks. It is far too great a burden to carry the emotional weight of my resentments, worry, anger, or sadness. I'd much rather humble myself and understand the lesson being asked of me.

The moment I consciously choose to grow, I feel a wise, calming presence soothe my mind and body. This expansive light helps me to reconnect to my highest self and gently reminds me *that on a Soul level, I am okay.*

In being connected to my Soul, I grow stronger within. From here, I am receptive and open to looking at my challenges from a neutral, wise perspective. In this healing space - peace and serenity flow through me. And in no longer being blinded by my current challenge, I can feel the essence of love *within* my obstacle, and I trust that it is happening for my highest good (even though it is hard). From here, I ask myself Soul level questions ...

Shortly, I will take you through an exercise to guide you through a similar process, and I will also give you the Soul level questions to ask yourself, **but first I want to invite you to open up to the possibility that there is a place within you that is whole, unhurt, undamaged, and unwounded.**

I believe our Soul is the part of ourselves that has not been hurt or damaged in any way.

Having spent a great deal of my life immersed in nature and feeling an eternal presence and expansive light emanating within all things ... having trained in mindbody healing modalities such as cranial sacral therapy and myofascial release and learning to work in harmony with the intelligent energy that gives life to our bodies ... through practicing meditation and being a student and teacher of it ... having spent years guiding my clients through mindbody coaching techniques where they can access their Soul's wisdom within their past pain ... through all of these unique explorations into the mysteries of consciousness, I have come to feel on a deep level that the Light of our Souls is eternal and has not been damaged in any way.

Without being able to know for certain - why do I sense that our Souls have not been wounded?

I would say after working with thousands of people over the past two decades, being able to sense that our Souls are undamaged is a deeper knowing, as well as a felt experience. When I feel the loving presence of my Soul, as well as others I'm working with, this expansive, eternal light does not feel wounded. On the contrary it feels whole, pure, wise, powerful, and infinitely loving. I do not sense pain or protection on this level of consciousness ... it seems to exist beyond the realm of defensiveness, darkness, suffering, and duality.

Now, respectfully, I don't suggest that you take my belief as truth. Instead, I invite you to be open to exploring the consciousness of your higher self—and in practicing to connect with the presence of your Soul—see if you can sense if there is a part of you that feels undamaged, unwounded, and is emanating pure love.

It has been said by numerous spiritual teachers in the past that we are spiritual beings having a temporary human experience and that our Souls have come to Earth, to duality, to learn and evolve in love. This resonates with me on a deep level. But, even if this is wrong, or if you are an atheist, what options do we *ultimately have regarding how to effectively approach life's many challenging experiences? How do we circumvent being beaten down or left worse for wear by enduring so many earthly hardships?*

Logically, it seems we have two choices …

We can respond to difficult situations by being stubborn, resisting what is, thinking our way is right, that life is unfair, that other people are wrong, or by being overly hard on ourselves (yet in so doing suffer the consequences of our own limitations, resentments, and blind spots). Or we have the option to humble ourselves, see our adversities as temporary, explore new perspectives, discover hidden opportunities, and ascertain invaluable insights into ourselves and other people (and in so doing transform our pain into purpose, our wounds into wisdom, and our blocks into rungs on a ladder on which we climb).

In light of these two options, do you currently have a challenge you'd like to discover a higher solution to? Let's explore that now in our last exercise of the *Anchoring into Grace Method*.

Step 9: Come From the Level of Your Soul

Directions:

1. This exercise will take about 10 - 20 minutes.
2. A guided audio of Step 9 is available at belladodds. com/peace, which I would recommend that you listen to in order to be supported and get the most out of this exercise.
3. In doing this exercise—practice having a greater desire to learn and grow—over staying stuck in your polarized perception of what is right or wrong.
4. Be kind to yourself in this process. If you have trouble seeing a higher perspective, ask a friend or someone you trust what lesson they see within your obstacle, pain, or challenge.
5. If you are experiencing panic attacks, PTSD, or struggling with a mental health disorder, I'd suggest doing this exercise with your mental healthcare provider. If you choose to do this exercise on your own, select a challenge that does not have a high emotional charge to it. In other words, choose something simple and manageable that you feel safe exploring on your own. (Just know you can stop at any time if it becomes too triggering for you.)

Part 1: Get Curious and Reflect on These Questions

- What is currently causing me stress, pain, or frustration in my life?
- What situation do I want to find a healing solution to?
- What current challenge do I want to handle differently or explore on a Soul level?

Write down your current challenge or obstacle that you'd like to work on:

Part 2: See Your Challenge Through the Lens of Wisdom

If you'd like to be gently guided through this mindbody coaching exercise please go to: belladodds.com/peace. Being guided through can help you to access your higher mind and wisdom more easily.

Take a nice deep breath in and close your eyes …

See a beautiful, expansive light in front of you.

Feel how this beautiful, calming light emanates a kind presence.

Feel its loving, comforting energy.

Know that this healing ocean of light in front of you loves you unconditionally.

Gently open up and allow this healing ocean of light to gently and lovingly flow into your body, heart, and abdomen.

Allow this healing light to fill and overflow through you.

Allow this peaceful energy to bring light and healing to any area of tension, fatigue, emptiness, or emotional pain in your body.

Breathe in and allow this healing light to fill and overflow through you.

Allow yourself to receive.

Now see a golden beam in front of you.

Merge with this beautiful beam of light and allow it to effortlessly lift you upward into the sky.

The farther up you go the more peaceful you feel.

As you go higher and higher, you feel lighter and lighter.

Now you are looking down at the Earth far away from your earthly problems.

You are surrounded by clouds of light, and from this higher plane you can sense that all is well.

Here, surrounded by light you connect with your Higher Self.

If it feels right, you may also invite a teacher or guide to sit next to you.

This teacher can be a relative, a trusted friend, or a spiritual figure like Buddha, Jesus, or an Angel …

Trust whoever comes to sit next to you.

Now from this higher plane of perspective, open yourself up to learn and grow.

Move into the desire to expand your understanding and let go of holding onto your grievances so tightly.

Create space for wisdom and healing energy to come through and trust that this challenge is happening for your highest good.

Know that your Soul is unwounded and wants to learn this lesson.

Be open to the wisdom seeking to be revealed to you and open yourself to learn and grow in love.

Ask yourself these Soul level questions:

> *If this obstacle is happening for my highest good … how is it happening for me?*
>
> *If this challenge is helping to prepare me to be more mature and ready for what I most want in life … what is this lesson trying to teach me?*
>
> *What do I need to learn?*
>
> *How can this adversity bring out the best in me?*

Take a few moments to tune into the insights that come to you. Be patient … the higher wisdom is there.

> (Does the wise sage sitting next to you have any helpful perspectives to share?)

If this challenge involves another person, you might also ask:

> *What do I need to understand about the other person involved?*

What pain is he or she seeking to protect?

Is there a way I can communicate with him or her better?

If I could see through the lens of love - what would love see?

Breathe and soften your protective mind.

Be more interested in your desire to grow rather than your desire to be right.

Take 3-5 minutes to gently reflect on the healing perspectives that intuitively come to you. (Be patient and present with your spiritual lessons until you receive insights that help you to feel lighter.)

Part 3: Journal your Healing Insights

Journal the new perspectives and healing insights that came to you during the exercise.

Part 4: Put into Practice What You Have Learned

Be committed to implementing what you have learned while remembering to be kind to yourself as you start taking new actions.

Beautiful job.

* * *

Having a growth mindset requires trust in the healing process as well as patience with yourself.

Sometimes healing insights will come quickly and easily to you. Other times you'll need support from someone not immersed in your problem to see the bigger picture. When healing insights do come, you will often feel lighter in your body, heart, and mind and experience greater clarity on the next action to take that is in alignment with your highest good.

This is why you do the work. Healing insights are often calming, empowering, and enlightening.

What happens if you are having trouble finding any insights or higher wisdom within your challenges? What can you do?

If you are stuck or mired down in struggle and doing everything you can just to stay above water—you may have too many challenges to make it possible to see the forest through the trees on your own. Perhaps your relationship is on the brink of ending, your job is overwhelming you, your kids are going through a hard time, and you're having health problems all at the same time.

If you are going through a difficult time right now and feel stuck—that's okay. Sometimes when you are deeply entrenched in a challenge, and you can't see the higher lesson or a way through, it might be because there is more going on than you can resolve by yourself. (In other words, if you could have figured it out on your own by now, you would have.) It might just mean the wisest action you can take is to get one-to-one support.

I personally love getting support from others to help expedite my growth rather than trying to figure it all out by myself … especially when I can work with coaches who have been where I am and have healed and advanced their lives to the next level.

If you feel like you would benefit in working with me, you can learn more about my 8-week program on my website. If you are currently up against a big challenge—*take heart in knowing that this is not completely a bad thing*—as equal to the pain is equal to the higher purpose contained within it. After years of working with people from around the world, I can humbly tell you that within your greatest challenges is invaluable wisdom that can not only help you rise to the next level of your life and set you free, but can equally help you experience more confidence, joy, and grace in your life. What I've shared in this book is about ten percent of the work I do with my clients. In my private, practice we go much deeper. If you'd like to learn more, you can check out a video on my website where I explain my approach as well as read testimonials from my clients.

If finances are tight for you right now, I'm also offering a group coaching program where I will be taking groups through each of the steps in the *Anchoring into Grace Method*. (There is sure to be some laughter and lightness in the group work!) I'm also offering an online course if you'd prefer watching videos to refer back on to help you get the most out of each of the steps. Supporting you with various financial levels is important to me, so please check out these options if you sense it'd be helpful for you to have additional support to get the most out of this book.

If you are needing long-term support and finances are tight—I would suggest looking into attending Al-anon or Adult Children of Alcoholics meetings. From experience, I can tell you that these meetings can create miracles. There is something powerful in being with a group of people who are holding space for one another in love, respect, and shared understanding. You do not have to have a parent who was an alcoholic or addict to go to an ACA meeting. If you experienced a parent who was highly critical, emotionally unpredictable, volatile, abusive, absent, distant, or emotionally unavailable — any childhood repeating stress that left you feeling unsafe or unloved — all of the stressors can be helped in these meetings. You can find meetings happening all over the world and online at https://adultchildren.org/resources/find-a-meeting/ as well as al-anon.org (My advice is try several meetings until you find one you resonate with.)

Whatever you do, don't feel like you have to carry your burdens by yourself and figure it out all on your own. We heal through community. Reach out and open the door for grace to come into your life ... and it will.

There are always resources available to us when we are ready to heal.

How can a growth mindset help you to reverse your overactive survival stress response?

A core problem we set out to solve in *Anchoring into Grace* was how to self-heal your overactive stress response.

Now that you have been through almost the entire book (congratulations!) — let's tie everything you've learned together and do a quick refresher on the key components so that you can clearly see how developing a growth mindset is pivotal in being able to feel good as you move through your day-to-day life.

1. In the beginning of *Anchoring into Grace* you learned that humans have two non-negotiable survival needs: we have the need to feel safe and the need to feel loved.

2. If at any given moment—we do not feel safe, secure, and loved or we do not feel that we belong—it is very difficult for us to feel calm and at ease inside ourselves.

3. In addition, we were dependent on others for the first 15-20 years of our lives, and because of this, we developed an ingrained habit of seeking to get our survival needs met outside ourselves first.

4. When our needs were not adequately or consistently met in childhood—in response we developed innovative strengths to improve our situation to get our needs met.

5. Our strengths have helped us in invaluable ways throughout our lives; however, as adults, we can overcompensate and use our strengths excessively when we do not feel safe, secure, loved, and accepted (and unknowingly, we can work against ourselves).

6. The problem with requiring our basic needs to be consistently and primarily met outside ourselves first is that we inadvertently become dependent on others to act and be a certain way in order for us to feel okay. But being primarily dependent on the outer world to make us feel good, puts us in an un-winning position due to the universal law of duality.

7. Duality exists on all levels of the physical world, even down to the microscopic domain of electromagnetic energy. (Electromagnetic energy is comprised of two oppositely charged particles of light, which play an essential role in building the physical universe and binding it together). In other words, without nature's

existence of opposites, duality, and electromagnetism the entire physical universe would break apart.

8. When we pull back and acknowledge the natural world as it is, a world made up of a multitude of opposites, of attraction and repulsion, of safety and danger, of ease and difficulty, of pleasure and pain, of making people happy and disappointing them, of doing things right and making mistakes, of feeling supported and being let down—we discover that we cannot work hard enough to always experience safety, security, and comfort in the outer world.

9. If we try and live outside of this universal law and blood sweat and tear it to try and create a one-sided reality to avoid pain, discomfort, criticism, and rejection—we can suffer the consequences of our efforts and burn ourselves out trying to do the impossible.

10. Instead, we must evolve to a higher level of consciousness and learn how to embody feeling safe and loved inside ourselves FIRST.

11. Love and peace are *ever-present states of being* that are available to us at all times. Fortunately, we can be less sensitive and vulnerable to the world and people around us when we learn to feel a level of safety, security, love, connection, and acceptance inside ourselves (regardless of what is going on around us).

12. When we tap into the infinite well of love, light, and peace and replenish ourselves each day—we can move through the world feeling our true worth (regardless of if we are being rejected, criticized, or temporarily

failing)—and we can feel safe and secure (even when we are faced with uncertainties and the unknown). Moreover, when we strengthen our connection to the healing presence of love, we can experience new levels of joy, purpose, hope, miracles, and serenity in our everyday lives.

13. Lastly, through being stronger, connected, and more secure within, we can reverse our overactive stress response and begin to foster a growth mindset. In developing a growth mindset, we can learn how to grow in harmony with the wisdom of life and allow both our joys and adversities to bring out the best in us.

Developing a growth mindset is an essential component to your long-term physical, mental, emotional, and spiritual health.

Because growth consciousness is a pivotal subject in reversing your overactive stress response—let's take a few moments to clarify the undesirable results that occur when you perpetually come from a control mindset—versus the beneficial results that arise when you adopt a growth mindset.

If you habitually resist challenges in your life (big or small), and you are simultaneously unable to self-regulate and embody a level of love and security inside yourself, then this can leave you in a disempowered position where your well-being is determined by how people are treating you and what's happening around you. In other words, if you live from the outside in, it means that you are dependent upon circumstances to be a certain way, in order for you to be able to feel good inside yourself. Over time, this level of dependency can leave you feeling:

- Burnt-out and exhausted.
- Hyper-sensitive to the moods and emotions of people around you.
- Anxious and overwhelmed.
- Unseen, unheard, or unappreciated.
- Irritated, resentful, or critical of others.
- Fearful of what is beyond your control.
- Hurt and needing to close your heart or put armor around it.
- Self-conscious and lacking confidence in your abilities.

On top of this, if an event occurs that is not to your liking, you may respond by saying:

> *Why is this happening to me? How can this be happening again?*

> *I'm over this. It's too much!*

Everyday thoughts like this can signal to your body that there is a problem and in response your body can activate your fight, flight, freeze response to protect you. If this happens, your heart rate will increase, your mind will race, your blood pressure and blood sugar levels can rise, and a cascade of other biological events will occur inside you within seconds (triggering an over-activation of your survival stress response).

Comparatively, if you embrace the experiences life brings you (both big and small), and you are able to nourish your inner well-being and feel a sense of peace, lightness, joy, and love within you (regardless of what is going on around you), then more often than not as you go through your day you can experience feeling:

- Calm and clear in your mind.
- Strong and energized in your body.
- Connected to your inherent worth and inner-value.
- In tune with your intuition and your higher purpose in life.
- Safe and secure inside yourself.
- Capable and confident in your abilities.
- Compassionate and patient towards others.
- Inspired to grow and learn with life.
- Strengthened by the healing presence of love.
- Connected to a deeper trust and faith in life that everything is happening for your highest good (even when things are difficult).

Coming from this empowered position means that when an event occurs that is not to your liking, you are likely to embrace your challenges more quickly and explore the situation as happening FOR you *rather than to you*. Instead of wasting your energy in an inner dialogue that reinforces your grievances—you can shift into an empowered position and say to yourself something along the lines of:

I can handle this. The intensity will pass and things will get better.

Everything will be okay in the long run.

I am up for this challenge. I trust and know that this is happening for my highest good.

I surrender my human weakness and pray for the higher wisdom of Light to guide me and show me a better way through this temporary challenge.

In response, thoughts along these lines can help you to reverse your overactive survival stress response, and instead of impulsively reacting out of your lizard brain (your amygdala's fight, flight, freeze response), you can engage the higher reasoning area of your brain (your prefrontal cortex). From here, your breathing can deepen, you can be centered in your body, and you can think calmly and clearly.

Additionally, when you begin to strengthen your ability to feel good inside yourself (regardless of what is going on around you by embodying light and peace within you), you can move through your days with greater ease, cheer, courage, strength, and trust. From here, you can feel more calm and serene ... and when challenging situations arise you'll be strong enough to ask yourself:

> *How is this temporary obstacle helping to prepare me for what I most want in life?*
>
> *If I could see through the lens of love, what would love see within this?*
>
> *What empowered action do I need to take?*
>
> *What can I stop doing? What can I start doing?*

As you practice anchoring into grace, you open the door for a higher level of wisdom and support to flow into your life and you simultaneously create room for miracles and inspiration to be a regular part of your daily experience.

You are human. Therefore you won't come from a growth mindset one hundred percent of the time. When this happens forgive yourself and start again.

It is natural to oscillate between protecting yourself and seeking to learn and grow.

Why?

For one, as you navigate the world, your body and mind are constantly giving you sensory feedback about how you are perceiving what's happening around you. Or to put it another way, when you don't like something, you may feel a recoiling or tightening sensation in your body, or you might experience negative thoughts and emotions. **This negative feedback loop is not bad;** it is actually essential to help you safely navigate the world.

In contrast, if you didn't have a negative feedback system—and you perceived everything and everyone around you to be great and wonderful all the time—how would you be able to discern an unhealthy or unacceptable situation?

I experience feelings of resistance and wanting to protect myself on a regular basis (that's how I know I don't like something or perceive it to be unhealthy or undesirable for me). In fact, I don't know anyone or any of my teachers who don't experience resistance. The difference becomes how long do you or I choose to stay in resistance or self-protection? A few seconds? A few minutes? A few hours? A few days or weeks? A few years?

It is when we *realize* we are in resistance or protection about something that we can pull back and invoke our ability to choose and ask:

Why is this showing up for me?

How can I handle this situation more effectively?

How can I be more kind and compassionate to myself and others?

What do I need to learn?

What is the higher lesson being asked of me?

If you embody a growth mindset, can you equally allow yourself to stop, feel, and process your emotions? Absolutely. Living with a growth mindset does not mean that you aren't allowed to stop and process intense emotions or to take the time to cry, yell, and be upset. Actually, feeling the intensity of your emotions, being present, observing, and honoring the depths of what you are going through … *is a form of growth*. Comparatively, ignoring, stuffing, minimizing, stress eating, drinking alcohol, over-working yourself, jumping from relationship to relationship, or distracting yourself in any way on a regular basis from feeling the depth, pain, and rawness of your emotions—is the opposite of growth—it is avoidance.

Being present and feeling your emotions is healthy, and sometimes there is nothing like a good cry to honor and release what is really going on inside of you. Thankfully, there are many ways to be present with your emotions. You can hold them as you would a dear friend and allow your emotions to feel seen, heard, and honored. You can listen to the depths of what you are feeling and re-parent yourself by sharing words with your inner child that you wish you had heard when you were younger. You can hold a space of unconditional love and non-judgment as you allow your emotions to be expressed and pass through you without resistance. You can talk with your partner, family, or friends about what you are struggling with. You can journal and reflect on what your emotions are bringing up for you. Or you can let out a healing, guttural scream in your car to release the pressure! Any and all are healthy forms of being present with what is really going on inside you.

Whatever you choose to do, my advice would be to find a balance between honoring your emotions—and being mindful not to drown in them. Emotions are powerful. They carry a great deal of weight. In light of this, try not to let the idea of honoring what you are feeling become a crutch that gives you permission to wallow in your grievances, sadness, and fears for an *unhealthy length of time,* as this can lead to another form of control that unconsciously keeps you stuck and causes you to suffer a great deal more than is necessary. Be gentle, check in with yourself, and be honest with where you are. If you are suffering over the same emotional pains or perceived wrong-doings from others—for months or years—it is probably time to reach out for support.

The good news is the healing journey is one of the most beautiful and rewarding journeys you can take in your lifetime. Connecting to your Soul's lessons and discovering the higher wisdom within your challenges and emotions can transform your pain into purpose and bring renewed levels of joy, meaning, and inspiration to your life. So don't be afraid to *feel and learn* from your emotions … they are your teachers and they have something important to share with you. Or as Joseph Campbell beautifully reflected on in the archetypal wisdom of the hero's quest,

> *"It is by going down into the abyss that*
> *we recover the treasures of life. Where you*
> *stumble, there lies your treasure."*

How can we embrace the idea of finding the higher purpose of pain on a global scale in a world overrun by suffering, injustice, and corruption? How can we possibly apply personal growth concepts on a national and global level in a world that appears to be erupting at the seams?

I have been writing *Anchoring into Grace* during 2020 (a year that will live in infamy). Personally, what has greatly helped me to stay grounded and hopeful during these challenging times (along with the techniques I have shared with you in this book), is when I stumbled across the historical research of Neil Howe and William Strauss and their book, *The Fourth Turning*. In their research, they share an eye-opening cycle in human society (that can be seen throughout the world), which occurs roughly every 80-90 years.

I first learned of Howe and Strauss's work back in 2015. Since that time, I have readily observed their theories and predictions (which were made in the 90s) manifest in ways prior to 2015, I would have thought *completely implausible*. In this historically documented, reoccurring cycle, human societies experience a GREAT CRISIS where it feels as if the very fabric of a nation can be torn apart. During these perilous times, a country often becomes greatly divided; but in time, a shared crisis begins to bring the majority of people back together as the people strive to solve some of the greatest challenges facing their futures and way of life. The worst of what we have endured (since the start of the crisis in 2008 with the global recession) up to the present, is thoroughly documented in their research, as well as the *seeds of hope* that we are beginning to see taking root.

If you enjoy understanding history and how it relates to the present, the research by these two historians and economists may **give you a greater sense of hope, purpose, and resilience at this time, as well as help you to reduce your stress levels.** In lieu of going into detail about their research here, I wrote an article on my website, along with links to their book and interviews with the two authors that I have found to be helpful. It includes examples of past fourth turnings, such as the American Revolution and Civil War (which in turn led to evolutionary leaps in society, such as the birth of democracy and the abolishment of slavery). In exploring this repeating cycle of division, the rise of authoritarianism, and civil unrest that led to these evolutionary periods, perhaps it will help you, as it did me, to relate to the current challenges of the pandemic, the climate crisis, racial injustices, economic inequality, and the weakening of democracy, etc. from a larger perspective and a more purposeful point of view. If you'd like to learn more—this article is available for you at: belladodds. com/resources.

Everything I have shared in *Anchoring into Grace* is to a large extent what I cover in my first session with my clients in my 8-week program.

There is a great deal more that I could share on this pivotal subject of Soul growth and how it is possible to find the higher purpose within our deepest pain; however, I believe it is wise to learn from a variety of teachers. Each teacher offers a unique perspective, as well as decades worth of life experiences that can accelerate our healing journeys. Fortunately, there are a wide variety of inspiring teachers to help us be more emotionally, mentally, and spiritually fit.

Here are a few books that have left an indelible impact on me and that synergistically build on the concepts within *Anchoring into Grace*:

Dying To Be Me

If you only read one book from this list, *Dying To Be Me* would be the one I'd suggest. Dying To Be Me is based on Anita Moorjani's near-death experience in which she slipped into a coma when her organs began to shut down after battling cancer for four years. During her time in the spiritual realm, Anita experienced a magnificent light and indescribable presence of unconditional love. In her NDE, Anita had a life review and learned invaluable lessons about herself. From perceiving her life on a Soul level, she chose to come back knowing that her body would completely heal and that she would be able to live her life on a new level. After miraculously coming out of her coma and making a full recovery, Anita's medical records have been studied by doctors from around the world, and to this day, her case is viewed as a medical mystery.

A few years back, I took a workshop with Anita. During this program, she shared her belief that everyone's life's purpose is to first learn how to love themselves as well as to know that they are unconditionally loved. I agree with this wholeheartedly and have witnessed profound shifts in my clients when they feel and know the beauty of who they really are. Without question, growing deep roots into love is an essential ingredient in our healing journeys. (If you are overly anxious or have hypochondriac tendencies, I recommend starting the book at Part 2 when Anita experiences her NDE. Part 1 explains her story of having cancer that led up to her NDE. For some, this will be helpful and quite interesting, while for others, it could be too triggering or counterproductive.)

Proof of Heaven

If you have a scientific mind, you might enjoy reading *Proof of Heaven* when exploring the possibilities of near-death experiences. Dr. Eben Alexander was a Harvard neurosurgeon when he slipped into a coma after contracting a rare form of bacterial meningitis. Prior to his NDE, Dr. Alexander believed the traditional western medicine school of thought that consciousness was created by the brain. While he was in his coma, Dr. Alexander's brain scans showed that his neocortex had been completely wiped out (the neocortex is the part of the brain that controls thoughts and emotions and makes us human). The only area of the brain that showed any activity while he was in a coma was his primitive brainstem. From a scientific perspective, the brain scans showed that Dr. Alexander was not experiencing any level of conscious awareness, but as you can learn in his book, this was far from the doctor's experience during his time in the spiritual dimension. Dr. Alexander's case is also viewed as a medical mystery, as this form of meningitis is extremely rare. Only 1 out of 10,000 people contract it, and of those who do, 90% do not survive. For the few who do survive, if they have been in a coma for at least four days, most need round-the-clock care for the rest of their lives. Dr. Alexander's case is extremely unusual. He was in a coma for seven days, and not only did he make a full recovery, but immediately upon awakening, he was able to speak. The first three words he spoke coming out of his coma are life-changing if you fully embrace the depth to which they point.

A Man's Search for Meaning

Dr. Viktor Frankl was an eminent psychiatrist who survived

the Holocaust between 1942 and 1945. During this time, he lost his parents, pregnant wife, and brother in the concentration camps. In his book, Frankl describes life in the camps and the psychology of those who could not endure the tremendous suffering versus those who were able to find a higher meaning and purpose even in the darkest of their circumstances. Dr. Frankl observed that those who could find a higher meaning not only had a higher chance of surviving, but they were equally able to find a way to move forward with their lives after the Holocaust ended. *A Man's Search for Meaning* is a powerful read that may aid you well if you are going through a challenging time.

The Power of Now

If you would like to learn to connect with the presence of your Soul, *The Power of Now* by Eckhart Tolle, holds this frequency beautifully. It is a wonderful book to deepen your spiritual connection, and Tolle can help you connect to feeling the inner stillness and eternal peace that is available to you at all times.

How Your Mind Can Heal Your Body

Dr. David Hamilton is a wonderful teacher who I was fortunate to meet and take a workshop with in London back in 2010. Formerly a molecular biologist, Dr. Hamilton used to spend hours in the lab creating drugs for the pharmaceutical companies. Over time however, he grew more interested in how the placebo effect could at times be just as powerful (and sometimes more effective) as the drugs he was testing in his clinical trials. Dr. Hamilton's research sheds light on the profound capability of our mind's ability to heal the body and reveals through scientific studies the pharmaceutical producing facility that we each hold within ourselves. *How Your Mind Can Heal Your Body* is an inspiring and eye-opening read.

Left To Tell
This profound and humbling book by Immaculée Ilibagiza shares her astounding experience of how she survived the Rwandan genocide and the deaths of her parents and two siblings. If you struggle with trauma that has happened in your past, reading Immaculée's journey of forgiveness and her power of faith may leave an indelible impact upon you as it did on me. *Left to Tell* is hard to put down once you begin.

The Adrenal Thyroid Revolution
If you don't feel like yourself anymore and are struggling with five or more unrelated health problems such as fatigue, stubborn weight, headaches, anxiety, depression, PMS, chronic yeast or urinary tract infections, hormonal imbalances, IBS, eczema, psoriasis, acid reflux, hair loss, insomnia, infertility, pre-diabetes, chronic pain, etc., *The Adrenal Thyroid Revolution*, by Dr. Aviva Romm is an invaluable read for your health and well-being. Dr. Romm explains why such a wide variety of symptoms are interconnected and what you can do about it to take your health back.

In addition to her book, I also recommend getting a blood IgG food antibodies test. I had unsuspecting food allergies to things like ginger, rice, garbanzo beans, and safflower oil, as well as common allergies to foods like gluten, cow dairy, and chicken eggs. (All of which were causing my body to have a daily, systemic inflammatory response—resulting in a myriad of painful health challenges.) In taking these foods out of my diet, my symptoms such as eczema, arthritis, bouts of deep sadness, fatigue, food cravings, PMS, and chronic pain (most of which came on suddenly) quickly resolved. I'm in my 40s, but after taking these foods out of my diet, my health and energy levels have improved tenfold, and I feel like I did in my 30s. It was not difficult for me to exchange rice with cauliflower rice and find other creative alternatives for my allergies when I felt full of life and like myself again—and the good news is it is not forever. When my gut heals, I can get retested and reintroduce some of these foods back into my diet. To avoid overwhelm, I'd suggest taking your food allergies out of your diet for a month. During this month, observe any health benefits you experience; notice if feeling better outweighs the inconveniences that can arise in changing your diet.

The Light Between Us

If you are struggling with grief, you may find great comfort in this book by Laura Lynne Jackson. I came across it on Audible and decided to give it a go upon reading all the rave reviews. After listening to her book, I took a workshop with Laura in 2016, and it was an unforgettable weekend. I am deeply grateful to have stumbled upon her work and have passed Laura's book on to many of my clients who have lost a loved one. I've witnessed my clients find deep healing as well as a beautiful shift in the trajectory of their lives after reading *The Light Between Us*.

I have other book recommendations that I'd love to share. You can go to my website for the full list if you'd like more titles around the subject of health, healing, the mindbody connection, and personal growth.

Closing thoughts

I want to thank you for allowing me to walk side by side with you on your healing journey. It is a great honor and privilege to share this journey with you and one that I do not take lightly.

It is one of my life's greatest joys to explore healing energy and pass on what I have learned. I will continue to share more techniques with you through breathing exercises, meditation practices, as well as different coaching techniques to help you balance your mind and uncover the wisdom within your daily challenges. This will be an ongoing conversation and exploration, and if you'd like to join me, you can go to my website where I will be uploading new videos and supportive resources for you on a continual basis.

My hope for you after reading *Anchoring into Grace* is that you have been able to see and value yourself from a new light and on a new level. A client I recently started working with put it beautifully when she said,

> "Evolutionary dependency is a much different way
> of working with my younger self. In other therapies,
> I looked at my younger self as being hurt and
> weakened, but now I see her as much stronger than I
> realized. Actually, my younger self was remarkable."

Yes, your younger self was remarkable. And your adult self is remarkable too. We are often so hard on ourselves … but life is challenging enough to not be on our own sides.

What might happen if you work through the steps in this book, own your strengths unapologetically, and give yourself credit where credit is due?

What if you understand the deeper reasons for *why* you're

being overly-critical, a perfectionist, people pleaser, rescuer, or an escapist—and lovingly and consciously work to bring your strengths into balance?

What if you stop putting all your focus on people and the world around you, and instead, strengthen your connection to the healing presence of unconditional love and peace that is always available to you? What if you quiet down that inner critic and turn up the volume on your inner warrior?

The journey of life on Earth is certainly an adventure, and it can be a great deal more fun when you up-level how you play the game.

It certainly *is* a wild ride down here.

Some days can be beautiful beyond measure, some may be calm and ordinary, while other days can be exhausting and absolutely heart-wrenching.

Like the ocean, the weather patterns change from day to day. In order to be equipped for what the seasons bring and to be the person you want to be in your life—remind yourself often that **taking time to reset and refuel yourself is not being selfish—it is being wise.** When you make your mental, emotional, physical, and spiritual well-being a priority—it will not only help you to be your best self—but it will equally help you to be your best self with others too.

Some of life's lessons will be harder than others.

And I know it can be overwhelming and heart-crushing at times.

Trust me I know.

I've been there too.

Life can be brutal and beyond painful.

But do not lose hope—or your courage—on your journey up life's great mountain. Sometimes the climb will be steep and ragged. Other times you will be rewarded with the most awe-inspiring views or a lovely golden-lit stroll.

Take heart in knowing that peace can be your companion.

Gain strength in knowing that love can sustain you on your hard days, giving you the courage to put one foot in front of the other. And just as grace can lighten your burdens, it can equally bring immeasurable joy and radiance to the simple moments in your everyday life.

You, my beautiful reader, are not doing it all on your own. *Not really.*

It is not all up to you. *(Even though it may feel that way at times.)*

Connect to love and peace more often and allow these healing energies to support you with grace … *and they will.*

> *"There is always light, if only we're brave enough to see it.
> If only we're brave enough to be it."*
>
> Amanda Gorman

For now, I will close by saying …

The healing wisdom of the universe is inside you.

My hope for you is that you give yourself permission to take time each day to remember who you are, to rest in love, to rest in eternity, and to allow yourself to expand and be replenished by an ocean of peace that is always available to you.

This healing light will give you the strength and wisdom you need on your journey.

Please keep close to your heart that as you take this journey you will not be alone. I and many others will be out there weathering the oceans and climbing the mountains with you.

See you out there, beautiful Soul …

All my love,

Bella xo

Acknowledgments

This book could not have been written without the unconditional love and support of my mother, Allyson. Mom, your belief in me, and the knowing that you were (and forever will be) in my corner gave me the strength and confidence to step off the safe and traditional path in my career and in life. How can I properly say *thank you* when those two words simply don't do justice? I will keep trying to thank you, not just with words, but with actions, big and small. I will forever strive to pass on to others the unconditional love you have given me. Thank you for teaching me what type of woman, friend, humanitarian, and person I want to be in this world, and the type of mom I hope to someday become.

Thank you to my father, who is a true warrior. Dad, thank you for making sure I had the best childhood, for your kindness, love of nature, courage, and indomitable spirit. Thank you for loving our family the way you do and for helping to bring out the very best in me.

Thank you to my beloved grandmother. Grandma, you are my role model and confidant. Your strength, grace, and steady poise are my inspiration. I've learned more from you than you will ever know. When I count my blessings, I count you twice and will do so always and forever.

Thank you to my dearest friends Tanya and Nan for your hours of guidance, helping me bring this book to life. Thank you for laughing with me and helping me to approach it from different angles when I needed to. It truly takes a village, and

I wouldn't have been able to endure the challenges of 2020 and writing this book without your generosity, love, humor, encouragement, and support.

Thank you to Amy, Kelsey, Cassidy, Matt, Angela, Maura, Kirsten, Thomas, Anna, and to my beloved bro Justini. Each one of you supported me in different ways throughout this process and gave me the fuel and joy I needed to finish this book. I am forever grateful for our laughter and friendship.

Thank you to my clients who have shared with me your trust, courage, and willingness to go deep. Thank you for showing up with all that you are. *Anchoring into Grace* most certainly could not have been written without you. Walking side-by-side with you on your healing journeys is one of my life's greatest privileges and blessings, and I hold each one of you in gratitude.

Thank you to all of my mentors, spiritual teachers, and to the countless courageous authors and inspired scientists whom have dedicated themselves to illuminating and understanding the mind-body-spirit health connection. Each one of you played an invaluable role in this book.

Thank you to my teacher, the Light within all things. You are my guide, you are my home, you are beautiful beyond description. I love you with all that I am. To nature, I hope to find ways to give back and help you in all the ways that you have helped me. You are my Bigger Why.

References

Chapter One

Sapolsky, R. (2008). *Stress: Portrait of a Killer*. Explains the deadly consequences of prolonged stress. National Geographic documentary.

Chapter Two

Lipton, B.H. (2008). *Biology of Belief: Unleashing the Power of Consciousness, Matter & Miracles*. Hay House. 136.

Chapter Three

Baird, J. (2018). *No Mud, No Lotus*. Onward: Cultivating Emotional Intelligence. https://www.onwardthebook.com/no-mud-no-lotus/

Chapter Seven

Hawking, S. (1996). *The Illustrated a Brief History of Time*. Bantam Books. 82-85.

Chapter Eight

Chopra, D., O'Brien, C. (2015). *Your Being is Beyond Time, says Deepak. Whoa, says Conan*. Team Coco. https://teamcoco.com/video/deepak-chopra-time-space

Fraknoi, A. (2007). *Light as a Cosmic Time Machine*. PBS. https://www.pbs.org/seeinginthedark/astronomy-topics/light-as-a-cosmic-time-machine.html

Siegel, E. (2016). *How Do Photons Experience Time?* Forbes. https://www.forbes.com/sites/startswithabang/2016/09/30/how-do-photons-experience-time/?sh=5fa9dd40278d

Hamilton, D.R. (2009). *How Your Mind Can Heal Your Body*. Hay House. 5

Steinhubl, S.R., Wineinger, N.E., Patel, S., Boeldt, D.L., Mackellar, G., Porter, V., Redmond, J.T., Muse, E.D., Nicholson, L., Chopra, D., & Topol, E.J. (2015). *Cardiovascular and Nervous System Changes During Meditation*. Frontiers in Human Neuroscience. https://www.frontiersin.org/articles/10.3389/fnhum.2015.00145/full

Epel, E. S., Puterman, E., Lin, J., Blackburn, E.H., Lum, P.Y., Beckmann, N. D., Zhu, J., Lee, E., Gilbert, A., Rissman, R.A., Tanzi, R.E., & Schadt, E.E. (2016). *Meditation and Vacation Effects Have an Impact on Disease-Associated Molecular Phenotypes*. Translational Psychiatry. https://www.nature.com/articles/tp2016164

Barbor, C. (2001). *The Science of Meditation: Meditation May Help Squash Anxiety. The Practice Brings About Dramatic Effects in as Little as a 10-minute Session*. Psychology Today. https://www.psychologytoday.com/intl/articles/200105/the-science-meditation

Romm, A. (2017). *The Adrenal Thyroid Revolution: A Proven 4-Week Program to Rescue Your Metabolism, Hormones, Mind & Mood*. Harper One. 35-38

Kabat-Zinn (2018). *Falling Awake: How to Practice Mindfulness in Everyday Life*. Hachette Book Group, Inc.

Chapter Ten

Sangerma, E. (2020). *The Ultimate Guide to Cold Showers: What Science Has to Say About It and 4 Easy Steps to Get You Started*. https://medium.com/the-ascent/the-ultimate-guide-to-cold-showers-44c7878c539e

Uvnäs-Moberg, K., Handlin, L., & Petersson, M. (2015). *Self-soothing Behaviors with Particular Reference to Oxytocin Release Induced by Non-noxious Sensory Stimulation.* US National Library of Medicine National Institutes of Health

Raypole, C. (2020). *12 Ways to Boost Oxytocin.* Healthline. https://www.healthline.com/health/how-to-increase-oxytocin

Young, S.N. (2007). *How to Increase Serotonin in the Human Brain Without Drugs.* US National Library of Medicine National Institutes of Health

Swaim, E. (2017). *10 Ways to Boost Dopamine and Serotonin Naturally.* Good Therapy. https://www.goodtherapy.org/blog/10-ways-to-boost-dopamine-and-serotonin-naturally-1212177

BrainMD, (2020). *7 Ways to Increase Dopamine, Focus, and Energy.* BrainMD. https://brainmd.com/blog/7-ways-to-boost-dopamine-focus-and-energy/

Alban, D. *How to Increase Dopamine Comprehensive Review: Low Dopamine Levels Can Lead to a Lack of Motivation, Fatigue, Addictive Behavior, Mood Swings, and Memory Loss. Learn How to Increase Dopamine Naturally.* Be Brain Fit. https://bebrainfit.com/increase-dopamine/

Alban, D. *How to Increase Endorphins Naturally.* Be Brain Fit. https://bebrainfit.com/increase-endorphins/

Chapter Eleven

Strauss, W., Howe, N. (1997). *An American Prophecy The Forth Turning.* Broadway Books.

About the Author

Bella Dodds has been in the healing arts for twenty years. She is a holistic health coach and meditation teacher specializing in the intricate mind-body-spirit stress connection. Bella currently has an international coaching practice and grounds her work based on four core pillars: to work in harmony with the wisdom of the body; to be humble to the mysterious, intelligent energy giving life to all things; to help individuals self-heal by transforming their pain into purpose; and to teach her clients how to reconnect to the healing power of peace, grace, and love inside themselves.

When Bella is not immersed as a student in the healing arts, you'll find her enjoying time with her loved ones, engaging in social and environmental activism, and playing in the mountains and oceans of this great Earth.

www.ingramcontent.com/pod-product-compliance
Lightning Source LLC
LaVergne TN
LVHW091215080426
835509LV00009B/1001